ndexing for Editors

£2
TBA
19/48

R F Hunnisett
n Assistant Keeper of Public Records

British Records Association
Archives and the User   No 2
1972

SBN 900222 02 6

TABLE OF CONTENTS

Acknowledgements   6

Chapter I: Introduction   7

Chapter II: Terminology   9

Chapter III: Places   10

(a)	Identification and Spelling	10
(b)	Inversion	11
(c)	Indexing Transcripts	12
(d)	Indexing Calendars and Descriptive Lists	15
(e)	Parishes as Index Units	17
(f)	Supplied Places	20
(g)	Corrections and Comments in the Index	21
(h)	Counties	23
(i)	Field, Street and other Minor Place Names	24
(j)	Subentries	27
(k)	London and other Complex Places	28
(l)	Rivers, Forests, etc.	29
(m)	Territorial Titles and Ecclesiastical Areas	30
(n)	Homonymous Place Names	32
(o)	Foreign Places	36

Chapter IV: Persons   38

(a)	What Persons to Index	38
(b)	Standardisation of Surnames	40
(c)	Early Names: Patronymics	44
(d)	Early Names: Servants	46
(e)	Early Names: the Use of *alias*	47
(f)	Early Names: Prefixes	50
(g)	Modern Prefixes, English and Foreign	51
(h)	Compound Surnames	52
(i)	Alphabetical Order of Surnames	52
(j)	Forenames as Index Entries	54
(k)	Forenames as Subentries	55
(l)	Relationships	57
(m)	Offices and Titles, Lay and Ecclesiastical	60
(n)	Homonymous Persons	67
(o)	Scottish Names	70
(p)	Welsh Names	71
(q)	Jews, Arabs and Orientals	71
(r)	Other Foreign Names	72

Chapter V: Subjects   73

  (a) What are Subjects?   73
  (b) Grouping   75
  (c) Headings   77
  (d) Homonyms   80
  (e) Persons, Places and Subjects   81
  (f) Subheadings and Modifications: Wording   82
  (g) Subheadings and Modifications: Alphabetical Order   86

Chapter VI: General and Special Indexes   91

  (a) General Indexes   91
  (b) Special Indexes   93

Chapter VII: Wording and Alphabetical Order   95

  (a) Wording   95
  (b) Alphabetical Order: General   96
  (c) Alphabetical Order: Places   98
  (d) Alphabetical Order: Persons   100
  (e) Alphabetical Order: Subjects   101
  (f) Alphabetical Order: General Indexes   101

Chapter VIII: References   103

  (a) Entry and Page Numbers   103
  (b) Volume Numbers   103
  (c) Footnotes   105
  (d) Important References   105
  (e) Consecutive References   106
  (f) Numerous References   108
  (g) Prefatory Notes   110

Chapter IX: Cross-References   111

  (a) General   111
  (b) *See*   111
  (c) *See under*   113
  (d) *See also*   113
  (e) *q.v.*   117
  (f) *Cf.*   118
  (g) Paragraphed Entries   118

Chapter X: Punctuation   119

  (a) General   119
  (b) Full stops   119
  (c) Colons   121

(d) Semi-colons 122
(e) Commas 124
(f) Inverted commas 126
(g) Brackets 126

Chapter XI: Typography and Lay Out 128

(a) Repetition by Typographical Symbols 128
(b) Repetition by Indentation 129
(c) Symbols and Indentation 130
(d) Paragraphed Entries 131
(e) Symbols, Indentation and Paragraphing: a Summary 135
(f) Small Capitals 135
(g) Bold Type 136
(h) Initial Letters 136
(i) Italics 137
(j) Space between Letters 138
(k) Run-on Entries 138

Chapter XII: The Indexer and his Technique 140

(a) The Indexer 140
(b) Preparation of Indexes: Order of Work 141
(c) Preparation of Indexes: Writing, Sorting and Editing Cards 141

Select Bibliography 145

ACKNOWLEDGEMENTS

Although the views expressed in the following pages are my own, I am naturally indebted to my many indexer friends and colleagues at the Public Record Office and to the general editors of my own record publications who have helped me to arrive at them. Especially I must mention Mr L. C. Hector, who has discussed editorial and indexing problems with me over many years, Mr R. E. Latham for kindly allowing me to include a summary of his hitherto unpublished scheme for indexing surnames and to comment on it, and Miss Barbara Eames, whose criticisms, based on her long experience of indexing, have improved nearly every section of every chapter. Mrs Shelagh Bond, Mrs Margaret Post, Mr J. McN. Dodgson, Mr Christopher Elrington, Mr M. W. Farr and Mr A. E. B. Owen read the whole work in typescript and made valuable suggestions for its improvement. I am particularly grateful for the trouble which Mr Owen has taken with it at all stages in his capacity as Honorary Editor of the British Records Association, and to the Association's Editorial Committee for their constant encouragement. I must also thank Mr William Kellaway and Dr Grant Simpson for their assistance, and Mr Peter Gouldesbrough of the Scottish Record Office for allowing me to quote examples of his recommended treatment of Gaelic and other Scottish names from his unpublished pamphlet 'Guide to Indexing of Record Publications'. Finally, Miss Elizabeth Stuart has been of great assistance during the proof-reading stages.

R. F. H.

KESTON, KENT
September, 1971

CHAPTER I

INTRODUCTION

The publication of records, central and local, public and private, can be justified in many ways, but most simply and overwhelmingly by reference to the footnotes in the serious historical works of the last half-century. The texts and calendars produced by the Public Record Office, the Scottish Record Office, the Public Record Office of Ireland, the Historical Manuscripts Commission and the many record publishing societies, and also privately, have extended the range and depth of historical studies beyond all measure by providing easily accessible information about people, places and topics which would otherwise have remained largely unused.

But a record publication is only as good as its index. A few users will read some volumes from cover to cover: historians of the baronial wars and reforms of 1258-1265 have to study the whole of the published texts and calendars of the Chancery rolls of those years; students of the Restoration require a similar familiarity with the *Calendar of State Papers, Domestic Series,* for 1660 and neighbouring years; and legal historians probably read all or many of the cases in the *Curia Regis Rolls* volumes. But most users of these and other series are interested in the relatively few entries which contain matter relevant to the more specific subjects of their research. There are often many classes of records in which the person, place or topic under investigation may or may not occur, or is likely to occur only occasionally or irregularly. It is not worthwhile for the historian to search the original manuscripts unless he has a firm lead; but if they are in print and properly indexed, he can speedily obtain all their relevant information.

That is why historical scholarship leans so heavily on record publications, and why their value is increased out of all proportion if they have accurate and comprehensive indexes. In this context the early nineteenth-century Record Commission volumes may be usefully compared with the corresponding Public Record Office publications: the *Testa de Nevill* (1807) with *The Book of Fees* (1920-31), and the *Calendarium Inquisitionum Post Mortem sive Escaetarum* (1806-28) with the recent volumes of the *Calendar of Inquisitions Post Mortem,* to give just two examples. The first, like most early editions of records, have no Subject Indexes or subject entries. They have separate indexes for persons and for places, but the places are not identified and modernised, and the variant forms of both persons and places, however bizarre, are indexed separately without cross-references. Thus a dozen references to a single person in the text can result in up to a dozen separate entries in the index, some perhaps adjacent, others well spaced, and possibly none of them in the form by which the person is generally known. However patient and ingenious the user, he can never be sure that he has found everything relevant to his interest unless he reads the text completely.

Indexes of persons and places improved only slowly during the nineteenth century, while, with certain meritorious exceptions such as the splendid index to the *Rotuli Parliamentorum* (1783; Index 1832), subject indexing is largely a twentieth-century development. Today all editors of records are conscious of the need for reliable and usable indexes, but it is unusual to find two indexes,

even in the same series, which have been compiled on exactly the same principles. This is because the indexing of record publications is a subject which has
hitherto been considered only very cursorily in a few short papers and chapters
and which most books on indexing have ignored completely. If all indexes could
in future be compiled and set out uniformly, it would be a considerable aid to
historical scholarship. It is the purpose of this work to discuss the principles on
which indexes to record publications should be compiled, to suggest solutions
to the practical difficulties which confront all indexers, and to recommend
rules and practices which it is hoped will be generally approved and adopted for
future publications. No single indexer would probably agree with every one, and it
is never easy to change one's practices, but the benefits of uniformity are worth
some small breaches with one's indexing habits. If it is any comfort, the present
writer has found it impossible to justify some of his cherished and long-estab-
lished practices and has been forced to recommend others instead. It is therefore
in a humble and not a critical spirit that this work is offered.

It is not a work on indexing in general. There are many such works, although
they tend to repeat each other. The most useful are listed in the Bibliography at
the end. Neither is this a work on the indexing of records, although many of the
recommended rules are equally applicable to that. It is primarily concerned with
the problems peculiar to indexes to record publications. Relatively little space
is given to matters common to all indexes, especially to writing and editing
cards, preparing them for the printer and correcting the proofs, which are com-
prehensively treated in most of the more general works. No space at all is
allotted to indexing by computer, partly because it is not yet clear what part, if
any, the computer can usefully play in this field, and partly because, whatever
functions it may take over from the indexer, the ideals to aim at will remain the
same and the principles and rules stated here will still apply.

This work therefore falls into two parts. Chapters three to six consider the
contents of indexes to record publications, the more academic side of our subject;
and the rest deal with the more technical aspects of indexing, whose rules should
soon become second nature, to be applied without thinking. The chapters in the
second part are shorter because, inevitably, many of the points they contain are
anticipated or exemplified earlier. Cross-references are provided to and from
such earlier treatment, and it is hoped that they, together with the very full
Table of Contents, will be more generally helpful than an index. Indexes to
works on indexing are traditionally either facetious or grossly over-elaborate, or
both.

A few basic principles may be mentioned in general terms at the outset,
because they should be borne constantly in mind during the compilation of any
index. A good index greatly enhances the value of any edition of records, but its
sole purpose is to facilitate the easy but reasonable use of the book as a work of
reference. It should not be a *tour de force* of the indexer's scholarship as such. It
should be as comprehensive as can reasonably be expected, but not verbose or
repetitive: no book should be rewritten in the index, still less rewritten in a
variety of different ways. Each entry should be simple and concise, and as many
as possible should refer directly to the text. Finally, the indexer must never
forget that, whereas he works from the text to the index, almost every user will
work from the index to the text: an index is not primarily for the benefit of the few
future indexers of cognate publications, but for the assistance of historians. All
these points will be illustrated and developed in the following pages.

CHAPTER II

TERMINOLOGY

Unfortunately the authorities on indexing have used different words to describe the same elements of an index, but the following terms are the most satisfactory and the most commonly accepted, and they are used throughout this work in the sense here defined.

Entry: The basic unit of the index, each entry relating to some place, personal name (usually surname) or subject, as defined in its heading. It should be noted that the word 'subject' is not used, as often, for the subject matter or concept of every entry, but is reserved for those which are neither persons nor places. Entries may be either

    (a) *simple,* having merely references or cross-references, or both; or

    (b) *complex,* having either or both of these and also subentries.

Unfortunately the word 'entry' has also to be used for those numbered divisions of the text to which index references frequently relate.

Subentry: A subdivision of an entry, introduced by either a subheading or a modification.

Heading: The main title or description of an entry, sometimes, but never here, called the 'subject'. Headings can be

    (a) *simple,* consisting of a single word;

    (b) *compound,* consisting of several words; or

    (c) *inverted:* compound headings, the order of whose words is changed to bring the most significant one (the key word) to the beginning.

Subheading: A secondary heading, introducing a subentry which is devoted to a limited aspect of the entry, whence it is sometimes called an 'aspect'. Subheadings are of the same three kinds as headings and may, in very complex entries, have their own sub-subheadings.

Modification: A word or phrase following a heading or subheading and limiting or qualifying it. A heading or subheading may have a number of modifications to break the entry or subentry up. Modifications differ from subheadings in that they cannot stand alone, whereas in a different arrangement subheadings could themselves be headings. Indeed, they may well so appear as cross-reference entries. A further distinction is that subheadings are frequently cross-referred to, whereas modifications can rarely be.

Key word: Sometimes called the 'catchword', this is the first word of the heading, subheading or modification, by which the entry or subentry is primarily alphabetised.

Reference: A number directing the user to a specific page or entry in the text.

Cross-reference: A direction to another entry or subentry.

Text: The body of the volume: that which is indexed. Because of this use of the word, it is never used in this work to denote the original records transcribed, calendared or listed in the volume. Texts of record publications take one of the following forms

    (a) *Transcript:* a 'full text', or verbatim rendering, of the original manuscripts, with all abbreviations extended.

    (b) *Calendar:* a précis, usually in English, full enough to replace the original documents for most purposes.

    (c) *Descriptive List:* a brief abstract of the documents.

CHAPTER III

PLACES

(a) *Identification and Spelling*

Place-name identification still presents many problems, particularly in the case of very early records and where constant copying by different clerks over many generations has resulted in extremely aberrant forms. Miscopying must account for the bizarre forms of place names to be found, for example, on Elizabethan Patent Rolls and in the medieval and later inquisitions *post mortem*, where a wrong initial letter in the original document can involve the indexer in hours of work.[1] Nevertheless, with the ever growing number of volumes of the English Place-Name Society and the Victoria History of the Counties of England, as well as better indexed record publications, the identification of English place names becomes increasingly less difficult, while gazetteers and works on the places of other countries are steadily being published. But irrespective of the ease or difficulty, or even the impossibility, of identifying particular places, the principles of place-name indexing are fairly firmly established. It is on these basic principles of indexing rather than the techniques of place-name identification that this chapter must concentrate. Because the great majority of places occurring in British records are within the British Isles, this chapter is devoted mainly to them, although most of the principles enunciated are applicable *mutatis mutandis* to those of other countries. Some exceptions are noted in the final section.

Every place name which occurs in the text must also appear in the index, where there should be references to every page or entry in which it occurs. There are only two exceptions to this rule: counties or countries or, occasionally, other areas or places, such as dioceses, mentioned merely to describe or define places within or near them do not warrant index entries of their own; and there are occasions, described below (III i), when field, street and other minor place names need not be indexed individually. Otherwise the indexing of places must be exhaustive.

Today places are generally indexed far more satisfactorily than either persons or subjects. This is because there is a single modern form under which the references to each one can be given.[2] The most up-to-date spelling should always be sought and used. For the majority of English and Welsh places this will be found in the Index to the most recent Census Returns, at present the 1961 Census. But for counties which have been covered by the English Place-Name Society or partly covered by the Victoria County History or the Ordnance Survey since 1961, the relevant publications of those bodies are to be preferred.

At one time hyphens were regularly used in such names as Spital-in-the-Street and Foston-on-the-Wold. Today they are rapidly dying out, and there is a clear case in the interests of simplicity and uniformity to omit them altogether, both from the modern and the obsolete forms (see also X a).

---

[1] For some good examples of wrong initial letters see the index to *Calendar of Inquisitions Post Mortem*, xv, under Belluton, Birdbrook, Bowden (Little), Burton Coggles, Catfield, Disley Stanley, Fawton, Netley, Rushall, Wacton and Walton.

[2] Until 1964 the Pipe Roll Society gave the references under the form occurring in the manuscript, the modern form being given merely in brackets, although it provided a cross-reference from the modern to the manuscript form.

(b) *Inversion*

In indexes to popular secondary works those place names which are qualified adjectivally are commonly indexed under the first word of the normal order, whatever it may be. Market Drayton, for example, is often found under 'M', as is justifiable in such books. But in record publications the practice of indexing such places under the word of substance is now well established. This is partly because in many cases the qualifying word was a relatively late addition, while in some it has changed at least once, usually when a new family succeeded to the lordship of the manor; but mainly because the retention of the natural order in big indexes would result in impossibly long strings of names beginning North, South, East, West, Great, Little, New and Old. In many place names, such as Newton Nottage and Toller Porcorum, the qualifying word is the second one, and so the natural order is retained in the index. But in far more the adjective precedes the important element, and then the order must be reversed in indexing, a comma both preceding and following the second word thus

> Newton, Maiden, Dors, 332
> Norton, Chipping, Oxon, 676

but

> Newton St Loe, Som, 517
> Norton Disney, Lincs, 23

the last two having no comma after the first word because there has been no inversion.

Inverted place names normally require no cross-references from the adjectives to the main words. In the vast majority of cases there can be no doubt which word is the word of substance, the place name proper, and which the qualification, but a few names are not immediately clear and require investigation. Hook Norton and Easton Neston are two such places: in fact, neither requires inversion. In any similar cases which require inversion it is helpful to insert a cross-reference from the natural order of the words to the inverted form. Similarly there are a few place names which have fairly recently changed from consisting of two words to a single word with the two elements running on, and *vice versa*; and others for which recent usage has not been completely consistent. They should be indexed under the form most commonly used at present, but with a cross-reference from the other. To give just one example, Kingsheanton should be indexed as a single word, with a cross-reference from Heanton.

There are three types of place name to which the normal rule for inversion does not apply. One is where the qualifying word is an absolutely integral part of the name. Thus Cape Breton Island and the town of Fort William should be indexed under Cape and Fort respectively, although capes, lakes, mounts, rivers and other physical features are indexed under the word following, for example

> Thames, river, 98
> Wight, Isle of, Hants, 167

Another is where the word which is qualified is obviously of less importance for establishing identity than the adjective. Abbot's Hall, for example, does not warrant inversion because the first word, although an adjective, is more exactly descriptive than the second[3] and also because the second, if used for indexing, would have to be used for very many manorial names. For the first reason New Forest, exceptionally among English names, should be indexed under New.

[3] In earlier times the first word was often used alone: e.g. Abbottes.

Finally, street names, field names and the names of other very minor places or features, which anyway are only indexed under the town, parish or other larger place in which they lie (see III i), are never inverted whatever the natural order may be. Upper Thames Street, South Audley Street and New Bond Street appear like that and are alphabetised, when necessary, by the words Upper, South and New.

(c) *Indexing Transcripts*

When the text of a volume consists of a full transcript of the original records, the place names must obviously be printed in the text in the forms in which they appear in the manuscripts. They are normally in the vernacular, but important places in early records are sometimes in Latin forms. All the manuscript forms must be indexed, the Latin ones in italics, with cross-references to the modern forms, except that manuscript forms which would be immediately adjacent to the modern forms need not and should not be included, as is explained more fully in Chapter IX. The references must all be given in the main entries, under the modern forms, which should be followed by all the forms found in the text in strict alphabetical order and enclosed in round brackets. To give a simple example, the main entry might well read

> Lichfield (Licchefeld, Lichfeld, Lyche-
> feld, Lychfeld), Staffs, 22, 78,
> 101-2, 234

It will sometimes be found printed as follows

> Lichfield, Licchefeld, Lichfeld, Lyche-
> feld, Lychfeld, Staffs, 22, 78,
> 101-2, 234

but the use of brackets is recommended. It is clearer, especially for places with qualifying words. Incidentally, if the modern form of a place occurs in the text it need not be repeated in brackets with the other manuscript forms. It is also recommended that forms of places identical except for one having a mark of suspension at the end and the other not should not both be included in the index, either in the cross-reference or in the main entry. Indeed there is no need to have any such marks of suspension in indexes at all: if a place name or surname is radically abbreviated that fact will be clear anyway, and if it is not abbreviated the presence or absence of such a mark is usually of no real significance, often depending upon nothing more than the clerk's feeling like making a flourish.

Our entry could give rise to the following cross-references

> Licchefeld *see* Lichfield
> Lychefeld *see* Lichfield
> Lychfeld *see* Lichfield

It is highly unlikely that there would ever need to be an entry

> Lichfeld *see* Lichfield

since it is almost inconceivable that these two forms should not be adjacent. Also one would normally be able to combine the last two of the likely cross-references to form a single index entry reading

> Lychefeld, Lychfeld *see* Lichfield

since there will rarely be an entry falling alphabetically between Lychefeld and Lychfeld.

Most of the better indexes have in recent years had the county after the obsolete forms of places in all cross-references. In them the last example would be printed

Lychefeld, Lychfeld, Staffs. *See* Lichfield

It is true that such entries make it clear that the cross-reference concerns a place, whereas without the county it might equally well refer to a person or persons with the surname Lichfield. But this is no great inconvenience when the indexer considers, and he must constantly remind himself, that well over ninety per cent of users will turn straight to Lichfield. Indeed, a considerable saving of space results both from the omission of the names of counties and from the consequent amalgamation of two or more cross-references which this often makes possible. Thus

Licchefeld *see* Lichfield

can serve for two entries, the place and a surname, while

Lychefeld, Lychfeld *see* Lichfield

is adequate if one of the manuscript forms is that of a person and the other the place. The saving is greatest for names such as Lincoln, where a single cross-reference can serve for entries relating to the bishopric, city, county, earldom and surname; and for very common place names such as Sutton, for which the single cross-reference

Sotton *see* Sutton

can cover not only the places called simply Sutton (and most counties have at least one) and the surname Sutton, but also composite place names of which Sutton forms the important element, such as King's Sutton, Long Sutton and Sutton Prior. Indeed, the same simple entry

Sotton *see* Sutton

can even be used for the obsolete forms King's Sotton, Long Sotton and similar places written with Sotton as a separate word, although not, of course, for Longsotton, which must have its own cross-reference under the letter 'L'. But the obsolete forms must always be given in full and uninverted in brackets after the modern form thus

Sutton, Long, (Long Sotton, Longsotton, Sotton, Sutton), Lincs,
29, 67, 144

Similarly, when a single obsolete form is common to two or more places which are spelt differently today, a single composite cross-reference will suffice, as in this example

Kyngton *see* Kineton; Kington

This is adequate despite the fact that the only Kineton in most indexes is the Warwickshire parish, whereas there are usually several Kingtons and possibly people of that name as well. Such composite cross-references are necessary even in a case such as

Alnewick *see* Alnwick; Anick

when the Alnwick entry is the next one. Without Anick no cross-reference would be needed, because any user turning to the obsolete form would find the identified Alnwick instead. But if he first noticed the cross-reference

Alnewick *see* Anick

he would probably turn straight to Anick and miss the Alnwick entry completely; and if, as is more likely, he had gone to Alnewick from the text and not found the 'correct' reference under Anick, he would probably conclude that the volume had been poorly indexed, as indeed it would have been although not as badly as might appear.

Care must be taken to ensure that obsolete forms common to several places are given in brackets after each, but that none is given after a place which it does not represent in the text although it may be a well-attested form of the place and found in other documents. Round brackets should only be used in connection with obsolete forms as above. If Long Sutton occurs in the text only in the form Sutton, it should be indexed

Sutton, Long, (Sutton), Lincs, 67

(with no cross-reference from Sutton even if there are other qualified Suttons separating the plain Suttons from this entry) and not as

Sutton, (Long), Lincs, 67

There would be no ambiguity in this case, but if

Norton Disney (Norton), Lincs, 19

were indexed as

Norton (Disney), Lincs, 19

Disney could be interpreted as the manuscript form of a place now called Norton.

Norton [Disney], Lincs, 19

is better, because names which are supplied are given in square brackets (see III f), but it is less satisfactory than the first usage since it introduces a separate type of entry just for those few places which are qualified today and occur in the text with their substantive element in its modern spelling but without the qualifying word or words. Other similar incorrect usages are set out below with the correct versions on their right.

Incorrect	*Correct*
Norton(e) Disney, Lincs, 19	Norton Disney (Nortone Disney), Lincs, 19
Norton Disney (Nortone (Disney), Nortonn), Lincs, 19	Norton Disney (Nortone, Nortone Disney, Nortonn), Lincs, 19

Apart from other considerations, the entries on the left are clumsy and potentially confusing.

Some may think it excessive to cross-refer from the manuscript to the modern forms of place names, in that most users of record publications who are interested in a particular place will turn straight to the modern form in the index and follow up the references in the text. There will, however, always be those who, while using the volume, come across a place in the text in a form with which they are unfamiliar or which they cannot readily identify. They can then turn to this obsolete form in the index to identify it. This is the sole justification for indexing places in the elaborate way described above. It may be argued that this usage is over-indulgent and needlessly wasteful of space, especially for places whose obsolete forms present little or no difficulty, as in the examples cited above. But full transcripts are normally made only of the earliest records, in which the obsolete forms are much more variable and often farther removed from the modern spellings than they are later. It is impossible to draw a line with any confidence and index the obsolete forms of only those places which it is thought might cause difficulty. The indexer should avoid having to make subjective judgments wherever possible, and while there will be some places in every volume which would cause no difficulty to any searcher and others which would cause nearly everyone trouble, there will be many in between which will be troublesome to some but not to others. The only reasonable practice to adopt is an absolutely uniform one. If all places are treated in an identical manner, the user will know precisely what the index offers and how it works, and the indexer has one less problem to consider.

Another objection to the recommended practice might be that, even allowing that there is some value in cross-referring from obsolete to modern forms, there is insufficient justification for printing all the variants again in the main entry: that this is of value mainly to place-name students, and even to them the value is minimal because they will still have the references to the text where they will find their obsolete forms and, moreover, will find them in their context and dated—information which they will surely need. A few other searchers may use record publications in attempting to identify a place, but normally they will only go to the index of a particular volume if they have some reason to anticipate that the place will or may occur there. They will accordingly expect it to appear in a form similar, if not identical, to that which is troubling them. This form, if it is in the text, will be in the index with a cross-reference to the modern form. Therefore such searchers no more need to have the obsolete forms following the modern ones than do any other users. Their omission there would be a negligible inconvenience, while it would result in a reduction in the size of the index and consequently in the cost of the volume.

This is a strong argument. The points against it are that considerably fewer records are now published in full transcript and that it is therefore late in the day to introduce this particular change in indexing practice; that the printing of variant forms after the modern ones would provide the main point of similarity between the treatment of indexes to full texts on the one hand and to calendars and descriptive lists on the other if the suggestions made in the next section (III d) are generally adopted; rather more tellingly, that when the county is not named after the obsolete forms in the cross-references, it is only by adding the obsolete forms after the modern ones that it is possible to distinguish the obsolete forms of homonymous places; and, most persuasive of all, that the searcher turning first to the modern form, as the vast majority do, will be alerted as to the obsolete forms he may expect to find in the text and so will not miss one because its manuscript spelling is aberrant.

(d) *Indexing Calendars and Descriptive Lists*

Most record publications today take the form of a calendar, and some are more summary descriptive lists. Present practice is still normally to give the place names in their manuscript forms in the text and to index them in exactly the same way as places in full transcripts. This is far from ideal. One of the main purposes of calendaring documents is to make more readily usable the essence of those whose every word is not regarded as sufficiently sacrosanct as to justify or demand transcription in full. But once one has broken away from a verbatim transcript, the purists' objections to translation, summarising and modernisation are broken. As long as the translation, summarising and modernising are accurately and sympathetically executed, the result is a useful work of scholarship. For the great majority of users its usefulness would be enhanced by giving all place names in their modern rather than in the manuscript forms. The only loser would be the place-name student, and he only to a very small extent.

The manuscript forms of the places need not and should not go entirely unnoticed. They should be given in alphabetical order in brackets after the modern forms in the index, which would still be considerably shorter than usual because there would be no cross-references from the obsolete forms. The place-name student would therefore still know what forms of a place occurred in the original documents. What he would not know would be at which occurrence of the place in the calendar or manuscript any particular form was to be found. The only solution to this difficulty would be to give the obsolete form in brackets after the modern one in the text, but this would be clumsy in appearance, detract from the readableness of the text, extend its length and destroy much of the purpose of the innovation. The difficulty, anyway, should not be exaggerated. First, if a place occurs frequently, it is probably large or important and its obsolete forms will already be known from many other sources. On the other hand small and unimportant places will probably occur only a few times in the text, and so the place-name specialist will have little trouble in consulting the manuscript (by photocopy if it is far away), which is something he would often need to do for his own satisfaction even if the obsolete forms were in the text. Secondly, many thirteenth-century and earlier documents are printed in full transcript. The great majority of printed calendars are, and will be, of fourteenth-century and later manuscripts, and by the mid-fourteenth century the normally occurring forms of most place names vary in no significant way from their modern forms. The main differences are the use of 'y' for 'i', 'k' for 'c', and so on. There is little profit to anyone to perpetuate these in the printed text. When unusual forms do occur, they can be printed in italics in brackets in the text after the modern forms, as must be done with those about whose identification the editor has any doubts, while completely unidentified places should be printed in roman type within single inverted commas; but, taken together, these should amount to very few indeed. Finally, the place-name expert has for long been spoiled by record publications, particularly official ones. The suggested treatment would leave him no worse off than any other user of such volumes, which would be more generally useful and less expensive.

It is true that under this plan the searcher with a difficult place name to identify would have less chance of doing this than with an index to a full transcript or to a calendar with obsolete forms in the text. But if he suspects that his place will appear in a particular volume, he presumably expects it to occur in a specific context: he will have some other lead, usually a person or another place, which will take him via the index to his place, identified, in the text. If he has no such lead, the volume would be unlikely to have helped him anyway, and his hopes must rest where he should have begun: with the volumes of the English Place-Name Society and other works on local topography. Nevertheless, for the sake of the place-name student the present practice—of printing only the manuscript forms in the text—is recommended for two kinds of calendars and descriptive lists: those containing records earlier than 1400, in which the manuscript forms are more interesting and variable; and those, such as editions of cartularies and collectanea, containing records covering a long period, in which it is useful to show from which years the various obsolete forms come.

What is recommended in this section is, of course, primarily a matter to be decided by the editor of the text rather than the indexer. It is one of many editorial decisions which have to be made with the interests of the text and index equally in mind, and it is therefore one of the many reasons why the editor and the indexer should be one and the same person, as recommended below (XII a). The examples given in the remaining sections of this chapter will assume that the imaginary texts are in the form of calendars with place names in their modern forms, which it is hoped will become the general rule for records later than 1400.

(e) *Parishes as Index Units*

It has become the practice in indexes to record publications for British places to be defined in terms of parishes: usually not the modern civil parishes, but the parishes as they existed in the middle of the nineteenth century. The justification for this is that, whereas during the last hundred years parish boundaries have undergone frequent changes, and the separation of civil from ecclesiastical parishes has introduced a further complication, previously there had been very little change since the early Middle Ages. By adopting the ancient parish as one's unit one is therefore choosing an entity which, with few exceptions, has undergone little diminution or expansion throughout the whole period from which records likely to be published in the traditional manner derive.[4] The only cases in which such parishes are not so used are for ancient cities and boroughs consisting of two or more parishes, when the cities and boroughs themselves form the entry heading, any of their parishes mentioned in the text being indexed under them as subentries; and for extra-parochial places which have to be treated as if they were parishes. These units—parishes, cities and boroughs, and extra-parochial places—are convenient not merely because of their long existence as entities, but also because there are admirable printed Indexes to the Census Returns of the mid-nineteenth century, in which the parish is the basic unit.[5] Because of these practical considerations, most volumes of the English Place-Name Society and the topographical volumes of the Victoria County History use the ancient parishes as their main units, which in turn aids the indexer.[6]

A few seeming absurdities result. Penzance, for example, has to be described as in the parish of Madron, while Edgbaston, now part of Birmingham, has to be indexed as a parish in its own right. The London suburban parishes do not have their references under London, as is explained more fully below (III k). But these are unimportant considerations compared with the overwhelming advantages which accrue from consistent adherence to the ancient parish as the index unit.

Parishes, cities and boroughs, and extra-parochial places are indexed in the simple form

Hemington (Hemynton), Som, 412

There is no need to put 'parish' or 'parish of' after the county, as is done in some indexes. Most parishes, however, contain within their boundaries a few lesser places which are nevertheless large enough to warrant index entries of their own. When such chapelries, hamlets or townships, manors and other large estates are described in the text in terms of the parish, they are easily indexed in the same way, for example

Highchurch (Heghchurch) in Hem-
ington, Som, manor, 24

[4] If and when records later than 1900 are so published, it is reasonable to prefer the most recent modern civil parishes as their indexing units, the *Index of Place Names* to the most recent Census Returns (at present 1961) or a more recent Ordnance Survey map being used to establish them.

[5] The most convenient single volume for England and Wales is *Index to the Names of Parishes, Townships and Places in the Population Tables of Great Britain* (1852), produced in connection with the 1851 Census. It can be supplemented by the fuller *Alphabetical List of Parishes and Places in England and Wales*, 4th edn (1897). For Ireland, the 1861 Census resulted in the very full *General Alphabetical Index to the Townlands and Towns, Parishes and Baronies of Ireland* (1861). There is nothing comparable for Scotland of a similar date, but the well indexed two-volume work of S. Lewis, *A Topographical Dictionary of Scotland* (1846) can be used instead. These are the works which have been used to establish what are, for convenience, loosely termed the parishes of 1851 in this chapter.

[6] The V.C.H. actually uses the parishes of 1831, while the E.P.N.S. uses maps of roughly that date.

with a cross-reference from the parish as follows

> Hemington (Hemyngton), Som, High-
>   church in, *q.v.*

With the obsolete form of Hemington correctly given under the modern one, it is unnecessary to repeat it under Highchurch, as was sometimes done in the spacious days of indexing and printing when the Highchurch entry would probably have been expanded to

> Highchurch in Hemington (Hegh-
>   church in Hemyngton), Som,
>   manor, 24

or alternatively to

> Highchurch (Heghchurch in Hemyng-
>   ton) in Hemington, Som, man-
>   or, 24

It cannot, however, be assumed that whenever one place is described as being near or even in another, the latter is the parish in which it lay in 1851 or even at the date of the document, or, indeed, that it was a parish at all. Thus Norton Conyers was sometimes described in the Middle Ages as Norton by Nunwick, although both then and in 1851 it was in the parish of Wath and Nunwick itself was in Ripon. The manuscript forms Norton by Nunwik and Norton by Nunwyk therefore necessitate the following series of index entries

> Norton Conyers (Norton by Nunwik,
>   Norton by Nunwyk) [in Wath],
>   Yorks, 345
> Nunwick (Nunwik, Nunwyk) [in
>   Ripon], Yorks, Norton Conyers
>   by, *q.v.*
> Ripon, Yorks, Nunwick in, *q.v.*
> Wath, Yorks, Norton Conyers in, *q.v.*

The last two entries may be regarded as the result of indexing the index rather than the text, and so they are. The justification for them is that many searchers are interested in particular parishes, and often in every part of them. Without the cross-reference from Wath to Norton Conyers, one of the main constituents of the parish, someone working on Wath might easily assume that the volume had nothing in any way concerning it and so would miss the Norton Conyers reference. But obviously the reference to Norton Conyers must come under that name, because it is the name which appears in the text and it is sufficiently sizable to warrant an index entry of its own.

When there are several manors and townships within a parish to be cross-referred to, it is recommended that they be given as a single subentry, as follows

> Tettenhall, Staffs, Compton, Pende-
>   ford, Perton and Wrottesley in,
>   *q.v.*

This is far more economical than the old practice of giving each lesser place a separate cross-reference in the form

> Tettenhall, Staffs, Compton in, *q.v.*
> Pendeford in, *q.v.*
> Perton in, *q.v.*
> Wrottesley in, *q.v.*

Another usage sometimes adopted is this

> Tettenhall, Staffs. *See under* Compton;
> Pendeford; Perton; Wrottesley

This is less exact, and '*See also under*' has to be used when there are references to Tettenhall itself. Rather better is

> Tettenhall, Staffs, places in. *See*
> Compton; Pendeford; Perton;
> Wrottesley

although the use of the word 'places' is infelicitous when there are other very minor places with their own references under Tettenhall—a subject which is discussed below (III i). The only disadvantage in the recommended usage arises when a place cross-referred to consists of two words which are inverted for indexing. An example is

> Hartburn, Northumb, Deanham,
> Greenleighton, Hartington,
> Middleton, South, Shaftoe,
> West, and Thornton, West, in,
> *q.v.*

But most people interested in Hartburn will know the chief places within it, while others turning to Middleton will find that the relevant Middleton is South Middleton even if they had not read on in the cross-reference and appreciated the inversion; and so, having followed up the South Middleton references, they will move on to the Shaftoe cross-reference, no doubt noticing the inversion this time. The qualifying words should never be left out of such cross-references, which should be exact in order to direct the user to the precise place, which may share a main element with many others—sometimes with others in the same parish, not all of which might be found if they shared a single unqualified cross-reference.

It occasionally happens that a place, usually a manor, which is large enough to have its own index entry, is correctly described as being in a place which itself was not a parish in 1851. It should be indexed as follows

> Lescudjack (Lescosacke) in Penzance
> [in Madron], Corn, 592

with the cross-references

> Penzance (Pensans) [in Madron],
> Corn, Lescudjack in, *q.v.*
> Madron, Corn, Lescudjack in, *q.v.*

If the volume had entries which mentioned Penzance in its own right, the second cross-reference would, of course, read

> Madron, Corn, Lescudjack and Pen-
> zance in, *q.v.*

Rather more frequently a parish or lesser place is described in the text in terms of a hundred or wapentake or other larger district, usually but not always to distinguish it from another place of the same or a similar name in some other part of the county. Thus Helston, which is in the parish of Wendron, is often described in early documents as Helston in Kirrier, Kirrier being the hundred, to distinguish it from Helstone in Lanteglos by Camelford, which was frequently called Helstone in Trigg. Trigg was the old hundred of Trigg Major, which is now split up with Helstone falling within Lesnewth hundred. These two places must be indexed in this way

> Helston (Helston in Kerr) [in Wen-
> dron], Corn, manor, 100
> Helstone (Helston in Trigg, Helston
> in Trigshire, Helston in Trygg,
> Helston in Trygther) [in Lante-
> glos by Camelford], Corn,
> manor, 531

There will be the usual cross-references from Wendron and Lanteglos by
Camelford, and in this case it would also be useful to have cross-references from
Kirrier and Trigg Major hundreds in order to identify their obsolete forms for
any puzzled searcher, as was done with Nunwick in the Norton Conyers example.
But when the Yorkshire parish of Hedon is described as Hedon in Holderness,
the only index entry needed is

> Hedon (Hedon in Holderness), Yorks,
> 32

because Holderness is spelt in its modern form and nobody would think of
looking up such a large area in the hope of finding cross-references to parishes
within it. For the same reason there is no need to cross-refer from hundred to
parish in those rare instances when there are two parishes with identical names
in the same county and it is therefore necessary to distinguish them in the index
by giving their hundreds or wapentakes in square brackets (see III n); or when a
place cannot be firmly identified and assigned to its parish, although the text
makes it clear in which hundred, commote or other subdivision of the county it lies,
in which case it is useful to index the place as being in the relevant subdivision.

Incidentally, before leaving our Helstone example, the modern form Lanteglos
by Camelford is so called to distinguish it from the other Cornish parish of Lanteglos by Fowey. Camelford and Fowey do not need index entries merely for
purposes of cross-reference to Lanteglos since they are integral parts of the
Lanteglos place names; although if Camelford occurs in the text in its own right
it will require the rather bizarre entries

> Camelford [in Lanteglos by Camel-
> ford], Corn, 196
> Lanteglos by Camelford, Corn, Camel-
> ford in, q.v.

since in 1851 it was in the parish of Lanteglos by Camelford.

There is one situation in which no cross-reference is needed from the parish
to a lesser place within it. That is when the two places share a name, or, if they
consist or one of them consists of two or more words, share the substantive
element of a name and are or would be adjacent in the index. Thus Ashton
Dando in the parish of Long Ashton often requires no cross-reference from Long
Ashton, which is, of course, inverted. But if other places in Long Ashton are
cross-referred to, Ashton Dando should always be included in the composite
cross-reference: not because its omission would be invidious, but because without
the cross-reference the main Ashton Dando entry might not be noticed if the
user turned first to Long Ashton and then to the places cross-referred to.

(f) Supplied Places

It will have been noticed that in many of the examples given in the last section
the parishes are printed in square brackets. That must always be done when the

lesser places are not specifically attributed to their parishes in the text, but have been supplied from other sources by the indexer. In most record publications the majority of parishes are not mentioned in the text and therefore should appear in square brackets in the index. Thus in the last example Camelford was assumed not to have been defined in terms of its parish in the text. The parish is accordingly in square brackets. There is still, of course, a cross-reference from the parish, since this is equally valuable, and indeed essential, whether or not it is mentioned in the text, the only difference being that there will never be an obsolete form if it is supplied by the indexer and does not occur elsewhere in the text.

Sometimes a lesser place is assigned to its parish in the text, but no county is named. The main index entry and cross-reference would then take the form

> Camelford in Lanteglos by Camel-
> ford, [Corn], 196
> Lanteglos by Camelford, [Corn],
> Camelford in, *q.v.*

the county being in square brackets in both because it is supplied in respect of both places. But when both parish and county have to be supplied the entries should read

> Camelford [in Lanteglos by Camel-
> ford, Corn], 196
> Lanteglos by Camelford, Corn, Camel-
> ford in, *q.v.*

It is unnecessary to have the first four words of this cross-reference in square brackets, because details of what is supplied and what is not are clearly marked in the main entry; and it would be positively misleading for square brackets to enclose the county alone, the implication of which would be that Lanteglos by Camelford was in the text but not Cornwall.

Every opportunity of omitting square brackets should be grasped. If a hamlet is stated at one point in the text to be in its correct parish and county, it should be indexed with no square brackets around either parish or county, even though it may occur in twenty other entries without mention of one or both of them. Similarly, there is no need for the county to be in square brackets if it is given in the relevant part of the text, although the parish or other place being indexed is not specifically stated to be within it. Incidentally, the frequent need to enclose the name of the county in square brackets is a further reason for omitting it from cross-references from obsolete forms of places in volumes of transcripts and pre-1400 calendars, as already advocated (III c). When the county was included under the traditional practice, it should strictly have been in square brackets after those obsolete forms not attributed to the county in the text, but without them after the others—an unnecessary complication for the indexer.

(g) *Corrections and Comments in the Index*

So far we have considered places which can be firmly identified and positively assigned to particular counties. But sometimes a firm identification is impossible, either because there are a number of possibilities etymologically and the context gives no help as to which is the place mentioned or because the manuscript form is too aberrant or illegible. When the place is utterly unrecognizable but the county is given, it should be indexed as follows

> 'Bercrcra' (*unidentified*), Notts, 24

This is more immediately meaningful than

> *Bercrcra*, Notts, 24

while

> *Bercrcra* (*unidentified*), Notts, 24

suffers from the defect of having italics used in a different sense for adjacent words (see XI i). The use of single inverted commas also accords with the treatment recommended for field and street names which have not survived (see III i). If no county is mentioned in the text, the index entry should read

> 'Bercrcra' (*unidentified*), 24

When the place must clearly be one of two or more known places, but there is no evidence as to which, it can either be indexed as

> Sutton (Soton) (*unidentified*), Lincs, 76

or, as is preferable when there are only two possibilities,

> Houghton Conquest *or* Houghton
> Regis (Hoton), Beds, 76

which has the advantage, in cases such as this one, of removing the entry from the unqualified Houghtons, where neither of the two candidates would be sought. Indeed, if there are Houghtons alphabetically between Houghton Conquest and Houghton Regis, it is safest to enter the place twice, the second entry reading

> Houghton Regis *or* Houghton Con-
> quest (Hoton), Beds, 76

In similar cases one of the possible places may be a parish and the other a lesser place. The obsolete form has then to be given after the supplied parish, as follows

> Denbury [in Ash Priors] *or* Durleigh
> (Dunley), Som, 26
> Durleigh *or* Denbury [in Ash Priors]
> (Dunley), Som, 26

otherwise the last entry would imply that both Durleigh and Denbury were in Ash Priors. Sometimes one can be fairly confident which of the alternative places it is, without having conclusive proof. This can be indicated in the index in the following way

> Houghton ?Conquest (Hoton), Beds,
> 76

There is no need to have Conquest in square brackets as well as queried, as is sometimes done, but the query must be adjacent to the conjectural element, and not to Houghton about which there is no doubt. By contrast

> ?Houghton (Hoton), Yorks, 152

shows that there is some slight doubt about the identification of Hoton as Houghton (it might just in the context be one of the Yorkshire Huttons, although this is much less likely), while

> 'Hoton' [?Houghton], Yorks, 152

means that there is a much higher degree of doubt. Entries such as the last require a cross-reference

> Houghton, Yorks *see* 'Hoton'

The form

> Houghton (Hoton), [?Sussex], 159

indicates that no county is named in the text, but that Sussex is much the most likely one, although there cannot be complete certainty.

The lack of a county is probably the most common reason for a place having to remain unidentified. If there is no possibility of even making an intelligent guess, all one can do is to index the place as follows

> Houghton (Hoton) (*unidentified*), 76

or, if there is even the slightest chance that Hoton might not be one of the Houghtons, but perhaps Hoton, Howton or Hutton, it is safer to leave it as 'Hoton' in the text and index it as

> 'Hoton' (*unidentified*), 76

When such an unidentifiable place occurs more than once in the text in more than one spelling, it should be indexed under the one which looks most modern, for example

> 'Hoton' (Hotona, Hottonne) (*unidenti-*
> *fied*), 76, 84, 177

with any necessary cross-references from the forms not chosen.

A suitable form of entry for places which were in one county at the time of the compilation of the records but are now in another is

> Ford (Forde) [in Thorncombe, Dors],
> *formerly in* Devon, abbey, 239

or, alternatively,

> Ford (Forde) [in Thorncombe], Devon,
> (*now in* Dors), abbey, 239

The Thorncombe entry will similarly read

> Thorncombe, Dors, *formerly in* Devon,
> Ford in, *q.v.*

Similar entries can be constructed to correct errors in the text, thus

> Chichester (Cicestre), Surrey (*recte*
> Sussex), cathedral, 59

or, less good,

> Chichester, [Sussex], (Cicestre, Sur-
> rey), cathedral, 59

and the same can be done in respect of manors formerly in one parish but by 1851 in another, or which are assigned to a wrong parish in the text.

(h) *Counties*

As already stated (III a), there is no need for a reference under or a cross-reference from a county when it is merely defining a place within its boundaries. References are only required under the county's name when it occurs in the text in its own right. Then the county should be written in full, either as 'Derby-shire' or, as is more customary, as 'Derby, county'. The only complications arise in connection with Shropshire and Hampshire. If the 'shire' form is normally used, there should be cross-references from Salop and Southampton, otherwise to Salop and Southampton. Southampton is the best illustration of why it is preferable to avoid the 'shire' form: by indexing under 'Southampton, county', one has the town and county adjacent in the index instead of far distant.

Indexes to pre-war record publications often have the county fully spelled out even when it is included merely to give a parish or lesser place a precise location. A typical entry might until recently have taken either of these forms

> Ingarsby [in Hungerton], Leicester-
> shire, 159
> Ingarsby [in Hungerton], co. Leic-
> ester, 159

But, as will have been guessed from the examples provided earlier in this chapter, it is advocated here that space be saved by abbreviating the names of counties when they follow place names, and so our example should read

Ingarsby [in Hungerton], Leics, 159

The abbreviations should be as short as is consonant with their being immediately recognizable and unambiguous. The suggested abbreviations for English counties are

Beds	Devon	Hunts	Northants	Suff
Berks	Dors	Kent	Northumb	Surrey
Bucks	Durh	Lancs	Notts	Sussex
Cambs	Essex	Leics	Oxon	Warw
Ches	Glos	Lincs	Rut	Westm
Corn	Hants	Midd	Salop	Wilts
Cumb	Heref	Monm	Som	Worcs
Derb	Herts	Norf	Staffs	Yorks

Possible but not recommended alternatives are Ex, Mx or Middx, Surr, Suss or Sx, and Westmor, but never Derby which could well suggest the town rather than the county. The custom of adding E.R., W.R. or N.R. after Yorks to indicate the riding is not necessary, except occasionally to distinguish between places with the same name. If the ridings were to be mentioned invariably, as they are in some indexes, it is difficult to justify the omission of the parts of Lincolnshire and even the divisions of those other counties which now consist of more than one administrative county. Moreover, the inclusion of ridings can create complications. Thus in our Norton Conyers example (III e) Wath is in the North Riding of Yorkshire, whereas the nearby Ripon is in the West Riding. This fact would complicate the Nunwick cross-reference. Altogether it is better, as a general rule, not to include ridings in indexes, especially now that the English Place-Name Society has published a composite index to all three.

The county abbreviations listed above require no full stops, whether they are suspensions or contractions. They are all manifestly abbreviations and will always be followed by a comma whether a numerical reference or a modification comes next. Similar abbreviations can be used for Welsh, Scottish and Irish counties, but in a volume devoted to English records with only a handful of references to places in those countries there is no advantage in abbreviating the non-English counties; indeed, infrequently occurring abbreviations tend not to be immediately understood.

(i) *Field, Street and other Minor Place Names*

The places smaller than parishes which we have so far considered have been hamlets, manors and others which are entitled to figure in an index as main entries in their own right. But others often occur in texts which are so small that nobody would think of looking for them in an index under their own names. Indeed, unless they are described in the text as being in some larger place, the indexer will be unable to identify many of them. But when they are so described or can be identified, such names of houses, taverns, streets, fields, small woods, parks, fisheries, streams and other minor features need only be indexed under the larger place, usually a parish, in which they lie. If the name has survived in a modern form, the most satisfactory practice is to give the modern form (but omitting such words as 'House' and 'Farm' if the place was originally larger but is now thus limited in use), followed by the manuscript form or forms in brackets, thus

> Coventry (Coventre), Warw, Hill
> Street (Hullestret, Hyllestret)
> in, 22

This agrees with the recommended treatment of place-name entries, and is therefore better than

> Coventry, Coventre, Warw, Hill Street,
> Hullestret, Hyllestret, in, 22

or

> Coventry, Coventre, Warw, Hill Street,
> 'Hullestret', 'Hyllestret', in, 22

The use of brackets is obviously much superior when two or more minor names are grouped together to form a single subentry.

Many minor places will remain unidentifiable, and they can only be indexed in their manuscript form within single inverted commas. If they come up in two or more different spellings, the one which looks the most modern should be printed first, followed by the others in alphabetical order in round brackets, in this way

> Northampton, Northants, 'le Oterowe'
> (le Oterewe, le Oteroue) in, 37

Inverted commas are not necessary for the variant forms: the fact that they come last, are in brackets and are obviously less modern adequately displays their relationship to the first one.

Quite often several minor places in the same parish occur in the same entry in the text. They can form a single index entry, or subentry, the names being listed in alphabetical order except that any article can be ignored for alphabetising without inversion. Such an entry might run

> Bryanston, Dors, 'Bradeley', 'la Com-
> be', 'Crofte forlange', 'Dame
> Sabynes', 'la Flexhey', 'la Gore',
> 'la Ladylynche', 'la Northfelde',
> 'la Park', 'Ridelond', 'les Ryg-
> ges', 'la Southcombe' and 'la
> Westcombe' in, 17

This is more economical than to give each field its own line and reference, but it might be reduced even further to

> Bryanston, Dors, fields etc. (*named*)
> in, 17

or

> Bryanston, Dors, minor places (*named*)
> in, 17

Strictly, of course, it is inconsistent to mention minor places by name when there are only one or two in a parish, and not when there are six or more. It is also in breach of the general rule that every place mentioned in the text must appear in the index. But strict consistency must always give way to common sense and economics, and even the most devoted indexer would presumably stop short of including three columns of field names under a single place. Even our Bryanston fields, if they were dispersed among only three entries, could give rise to an index entry such as

> Bryanston, Dors, 'Bradeley' in, 17
> 'la Combe' and 'Crofte forlange' in, 25
> 'Dame Sabynes' in, 17
> 'la Flexhey' in, 95
> 'la Gore' in, 25
> 'la Ladylynche' in, 17
> 'la Northfelde' and 'la Park' in, 95
> 'Ridelond' and 'les Rygges' in, 25
> 'la Southcombe' in, 17
> 'la Westcombe' in, 95

if one were to be absolutely pedantic about strict alphabetical order; or, more sensibly, to this

> Bryanston, Dors, 'Bradeley', 'Dame Sabynes', 'la Ladylynche' and 'la Southcombe' in, 17
> 'la Combe', 'Crofte forlange', 'la Gore', 'Ridelond' and 'les Rygges' in, 25
> 'la Flexhey', 'la Northfelde', 'la Park' and 'la Westcombe' in, 95

But even the latter amply justifies the further reduction to

> Bryanston, Dors, fields etc. (*named*) in, 17, 25, 95

It is all a question of balance, and if field names occur regularly and frequently throughout the text there is a case for having them in a separate index of their own (see VI b).

In some indexes the field and other minor names appear as a number of individual subentries under the parish, each in its correct alphabetical position within the alphabetical arrangement of the whole of the subentries. But, as shown above, that wastes much space when there are several such names, since they invariably relate to relatively few entries and so can be brought together into one or two composite subentries, which it would be slightly misleading to alphabetise among all the other subentries by the first place of each group. For this reason it is recommended that, except under London in most indexes and perhaps under the county town in volumes relating to a particular county— special cases which are considered below (III k)—the minor places, whether spelled out or not, should form the last subentry or subentries under a parish to have a direct numerical reference, being followed only by cross-references to hamlets and manors and to men of the parish, as in this example

> Coventry, Warw, 92, 154, 513
> inquisitions taken at, 11, 336
> mayor of, 663
> 'Chilternefeld', 'Chilternhull' (Chilternehull), Hill Street (Hullestret) and 'Muryholt' in, 245
> Cheylesmore in, *q.v.*
> Brown, Preston and Smith of, *q.v.*

If Hill Street had been in a different entry from the other places, the last
subentries would read

> 'Chilternefeld', 'Chilternhull' (Chil-
>   ternehull) and 'Muryholt' in,
>   245
> Hill Street (Hullestret) in, 116
> Cheylesmore in, q.v.
> Brown, Preston and Smith of, q.v.

The last subentry relates to men who are specifically described both in the text
and under their own names in the index as 'of Coventry'. More will be heard
of them later (IV n).

(j) Subentries

Except in General Indexes (see VI a), subentries of places should be kept to a
minimum, and as far as possible they should relate to persons and places. The
only subject-type subentries which should normally be found under places in an
Index of Persons and Places are those such as 'inquisitions taken at', 'letters
dated at' and 'writs dated at', which serve as a warning to the person interested
in a place that the references so distinguished do not relate very intimately to
the place itself, and also, being matters which could not easily be indexed except
under places, provide useful information for searchers interested in administration; and others, usually under countries, such as 'army of' or 'ships of', which
can usefully break down what might otherwise be an excessively long string of
numbers and are valuable in the context of the countries.

Places not so far mentioned which deserve subentries under parishes or
townships are religious houses, churches, chapels and chantries, castles, manors
when they have the same names as their parishes or townships, major buildings
such as guildhalls and gaols, and so on. Dedications of religious houses, churches,
chapels and chantries need not be discovered and included in the index, but
neither should they be excluded if they are given in the text. Persons to be
mentioned are all officials and clergy having a fixed relationship with the place:
mayors and bailiffs of towns, stewards and bailiffs of manors, abbots, priors,
rectors, vicars, chaplains, in fact anyone who is described in terms of the town
or parish—or of the county in the case of officials such as sheriffs, escheators,
justices of the peace and lords lieutenant. Exactly how such persons should be
indexed will be described in detail later (IV m). Here it will suffice to give a
specimen entry of a typical place

> Lincoln (Lyncolne), Lincs, 53, 229,
>   578
>   castle, 53, 578
>   constable of, 162
>   cathedral, 341
>   dean of, 129, 133
>   vicars of, 341
>   church of St Swithin in, 185
>   commission dated at, 278
>   Guildhall, 307
>   inquisition dated at, 32
>   King's Bench at, 497-500

Lincoln (*contd*)
mayor of, 185
suburbs of, 376
writ dated at, 341
'le Grenehull' in, 341
Wigford in, *q.v.*
Hurst and Nash of, *q.v.*

(k) *London and other Complex Places*

In many indexes London requires special treatment, as may other large towns in some indexes: county towns, for example, in volumes relating to particular counties. This is because they will need a larger than usual number of subentries, although of a kind occurring to a smaller extent under many other places. The general principles to apply are the same as for less complex entries: artificial subentries should be avoided, even if this results in a larger than normal number of direct references after the place names themselves; and the subentries should be arranged in alphabetical order, with cross-references to named places and persons coming at the end. But certain modifications to the second principle may be required. First, especially in the case of London, there will often be a number of people described as citizens, and others described as citizens and goldsmiths, citizens and skinners, and so on. If there are relatively few of each they can be given in the form

London, citizens of *see* Black; Twen-
tyman; White
citizen and poulterer of *see* Duck
citizen and stockfishmonger of *see*
Herring

in their correct alphabetical position under 'C' among the London subentries.[7]
But if there are too many for this treatment, such subentries can be reduced to

London, citizens (*named*) of, 22, 62,
105
citizens and goldsmiths (*named*) of,
153, 219
citizen and poulterer of *see* Duck

Secondly, it is often desirable to have subentries grouped together under group subheadings such as 'churches in', 'parishes in', 'religious houses in and near', 'streets and minor places in and near' and 'wards of', the dependent entries of each being in alphabetical order and the group subheadings being in the main

---

[7] Such goldsmiths, skinners, etc., who are usually described in the text in the form 'Simon White, citizen and goldsmith of London', are members of the City Livery Companies. They are therefore indexed in a different way from other people who merely practised a trade. 'Simon White of Hastings, fisherman,' would only appear under Hastings in the normal final cross-reference

Hastings, Sussex, White of, *q.v.*

although if he were one of a large number of Hastings fishermen the final cross-reference would be omitted, being replaced by the subentry

Hastings, Sussex, fishermen (*named*) of, 635

If there are unnamed fishermen mentioned, they will, of course, be indexed as

Hastings, Sussex, fishermen of, 635

The last two subentries would be alphabetically arranged by the word 'fishermen' among the Hastings subentries. More about occupations will be found in section IV n.

alphabetical sequence of subentries. A typical entry might begin

> London, 18, 56, 199, 637
>> charter dated at, 79
>> churches in
>>> All Hallows the Great, 22
>>> St Alphage, Cripplegate, 78
>>> St Michael, Wood Street, (St Michael in Hogenlane), parishioners of, 404
>> citizens (*named*) of, 993

and end

>> suburbs of, 183, 226, 337
>> wards of
>>> Aldersgate (Aldrichgate), 336
>>> aldermen of, 336-8
>>> Bread Street (Bredestrete), 225
>>> Castle Baynard, 289
>>> Dowgate (Douugate), 514
>> Buss, Cox and Wright of, *q.v.*
>> *See also* Charing Cross; Hampstead; Holborn; Mile End; St Martin in the Fields; Stepney; Westminster

The last subentry illustrates the third way in which London requires exceptional treatment. The cross-references are to parishes and other sizable or important places within the inner suburbs which are thought of today as being essentially part of London, but which are outside the City proper. The subentry replaces the normal cross-reference to manors, townships and similar places, which is not needed for London, and it comes at the very end, instead of preceding the cross-reference to named persons, because of its form and importance. Holborn, Westminster and the other places will, of course, appear in their own right, either as cities, boroughs and parishes, or as places within such, in the old counties of Middlesex, Essex, Kent and Surrey; and there will be cross-references under Westminster to the places in it which are also cross-referred to under London: Charing Cross and St Martin in the Fields in our example. It is not necessary to go as far as some indexers and have a single entry 'London and Westminster'. That breaks radically with normal indexing practice, while still leaving Holborn and other places around the City separate. A similar final cross-reference may sometimes be helpful under places such as Birmingham and Manchester, which have undergone considerable recent expansion, but London is the only place not indexed as in a county. Even places like Bristol and Newcastle upon Tyne, however large and autonomous they may now be, should be assigned to their 1851 counties.

Finally, Oxford and Cambridge often need a group subheading 'colleges and halls in', although if there are many individual colleges named and they require subentries, separate entries for 'Oxford University' and 'Cambridge University', distinct from the towns and placed between them and the counties, are preferable.

(l) *Rivers, Forests, etc.*

The general rule for indexing rivers, lakes, forests, mountain ranges and other similar features, usually of considerable extent and often in more than one county, is not to describe them in terms of a county unless it is necessary for purposes of differentiation. Thus

Ouse, [Sussex], river, 32

is a good entry because it immediately warns off those interested in the Great Ouse or the Yorkshire Ouse, and it may occasionally be necessary to define yet more exactly, as in

Rother, [East Sussex], river, 162

there being a River Rother in West Sussex as well as in Yorkshire. But when there is no possibility of confusion the county should be omitted.

Thames (Tamese), river, 193

is adequate, even if entry 193 concerns only a small stretch of the Thames, lying in just one county. Many volumes will contain entries mentioning various reaches of the Thames in different counties, and it would be tedious to insert a separate subentry in the index under Thames for every county mentioned, especially as many of the references might have to be repeated. Very few searchers turning in the index to the Thames will be interested in only one stretch of it. If the major rivers are indexed merely by their own names, it is reasonable that smaller ones which give rise to no possibility of confusion should also be, even when they flow through only one county. Forests, mountain ranges and lakes may or may not overlap two or more counties, but as they hardly ever permit any confusion among themselves they need never be described by counties. Indeed, there is much to be said for distinguishing them as markedly as possible from any places from which they derive their names, as with

Chippenham (Cippenham), forest, 46

contrasted with the parish

Chippenham (Cippenham), Wilts, 159

The order in which such homonymous entries should be arranged in the index is explained below (III n).

There are, however, some relatively minor features, such as roads, earthworks and small watercourses, which are of a size and importance midway between the major ones so far discussed in this section and the very minor ones dealt with earlier (III i). Although usually lying in only one county, they do not fall within a single parish and, indeed, often form the boundary between two or more parishes. Such features are most neatly indexed as entries in their own right rather than under one or more or all of the parishes they touch. It is unnecessary to describe them in terms of their parishes, but it is useful for the county to be given. A typical entry would therefore simply read

Hereward's Street, Derb, 294

without, of course, cross-references from all the parishes through which the street passed, or even from those relevant to the text as they will appear in the index with their own direct references anyway.

(m) *Territorial Titles and Ecclesiastical Areas*
Honors and baronies, liberties and franchises are other geographical divisions which may or may not be in more than one county and which are therefore usually indexed without reference to a county. Thus

Wallingford (Walyngford), honor, 22,
72

which honor extended into many counties, contrasts usefully with

Wallingford (Walynford), Berks, 67

the borough and *caput* of the honor. For exactly the same reason—that they are not geographically conterminous—the earldom of Huntingdon must have an index entry separate from the town and the county of Huntingdon, and the duchies of Cornwall and Lancaster must be kept apart from the counties of those names and the town of Lancaster. The argument for giving no county location and for keeping them apart from the county of the same name is even stronger in respect of those earldoms, dukedoms and other titles which are named after real places with which they have no geographical connection.

There are four exceptions, or apparent exceptions, to the above rule. One is that the territorial baronies of Ireland and Scotland should be given their counties. They should be treated like English hundreds. Secondly, the county should be given for all lordships when this term denotes lordships of manors, whether or not the word 'manor' is specifically mentioned in the text. If it is not, the entry should take the form

Bexhill, Sussex, lordship of, 621

Again, the county should be included after the name of any lordship or liberty which is a common one, such as Newport, to remove any uncertainty, even if the whole of the lordship does not lie in that county. The final exception occurs when a liberty is described in terms of a person who is himself described in terms of a city, borough, parish or other small place, for example

Battle, Sussex, abbot of, liberty of, 64

The liberty of the abbot of Battle consisted of lands in several counties, but as he was abbot of the abbey which was within the parish of Battle the above entry is correct. If the reference is to his Wiltshire lands, it is helpful to index it as

Battle, Sussex, abbot of, liberty of, in
Wilts, 64

otherwise the mention of Sussex might be misleading.

Whereas the liberties of religious houses are correctly indexed under the parishes or other places in which the houses were situated, provinces, dioceses and other ecclesiastical areas larger than parishes or towns require separate index entries and no county definitions, even when they are wholly within one county. Thus the diocese of Chichester is conterminous with the county of Sussex, but is merely indexed in the form

Chichester (Chichestre), diocese, 48
bishop of, liberty of, 732

There must be no confusion in the index with the cathedral, which is within the city and so must be indexed

Chichester (Cicestre), Sussex, 49
cathedral, 22, 88
dean and chapter of, 22

The fact that the cathedral is the ecclesiastical hub of the diocese and contains the bishop's throne is irrelevant to the indexer. Larger dioceses and archiepiscopal provinces are less likely to be wrongly indexed under the cathedral cities, although the dioceses of Canterbury and York are sometimes conflated with the provinces and should not be since they are geographically much smaller.

Archdeaconries and rural deaneries should not be given county descriptions because they are essentially subdivisions of dioceses rather than of counties. Indeed, they are sometimes found indexed as subentries of the dioceses, but they should have their own individual entries in their correct alphabetical positions within the whole index. Deans of cathedrals, however, should not be given

separate entries, but should come within the city entries, under the cathedral
subentry if there is one, as in the last Chichester example. Prebends and pre-
bendaries should be indexed twice when the prebends derive their names from
places and these are specified in the text: once under the places and again under
the relevant cathedrals, as follows

> Chichester (Cicestre), Sussex, cathe-
>   dral, prebendary of Selsey in,
>   772
> Selsey, Sussex, prebendary of, in
>   Chichester cathedral, 772

The second of these entries is particularly valuable if the cathedral is not specified
in the text, when the last three words, being supplied, must be in square brackets.

The secular and ecclesiastical titles and areas mentioned in this section sometimes occur in the text as such, but very much more often to describe a person:
a peer, bishop, dean, and so on. It is more convenient to reserve a consideration
of them from this standpoint for a later chapter (IV m), in connection with the
indexing of personal names.

(n) *Homonymous Place Names*

One major principle which emerges from the last section is that every distinct
geographical area, whatever its nature, which is the size of a township or manor,
or larger, should have a separate index entry of its own, irrespective of whether
or not it shares a name or has a significant word in common with other places or
areas, and whether or not it physically contains them or is within them: the only
exception being manors which share their parishes' names exactly. Secondly,
each entry must be a completely new one, and not represented merely by indentation from the shared name or by some other typographical convention, as will be
found in many indexes. In other words, whenever a place name's significance
changes it must be spelled out anew and redefined. This avoids any possibility
of confusion, ensures that an entry is not overlooked, and allows greater flexi-
bility for subentries since the first indentation or other sign of repetition will be
available for use under every place.

The order in which such homonymous places and places sharing a significant
word should be arranged is as follows: first, ecclesiastical areas in the order
province, diocese, archdeaconry and rural deanery; then any hundred or equivalent area, city, town, parish, township and manor, although not necessarily in
that order as will shortly be explained; county; any honor or liberty; any province, state or other foreign administrative area; next, any major physical
features—forest, lake, mountain or river, arranged in alphabetical order thus;
and finally any barony, duchy or dukedom, earldom or marquessate, again in
that alphabetical order. This is the generally accepted order, except that peerage
titles have been switched from first to last so that they are adjacent to surnames
of the same spelling which always follow places. That is a useful juxtaposition
in that family names of peers are quite often the same as their peerages. This all
looks at first sight more complicated than it ever is in practice. Apart from the
normal identity of names of county and county town, and frequently that of
hundred and parish or lesser place, it is parishes and towns which can create
the longest runs of homonymous entries. It is rarely that an index contains more
than one ecclesiastical area or more than one peerage with the same name. Two

of the more lengthy runs with different kinds of places represented would be

> Lincoln, diocese, 56
>> bishop of *see* Grosseteste, Robert
> Lincoln, Lincs, 137
>> castle, 77, 542
>> inquisitions taken at, 199, 542
> Lincoln, county, 335
>> sheriffs of, 578, 604
> Lincoln, earls of *see* Lacy
> Lincoln (Lyncolne), John, 271
>> Thomas, 381
>
> York, province, 677
>> archbishops of, 332, 569
> York, diocese, 542
> York, Yorks, 284
>> castle, 82
>> coroners of, 289
>> mayor of, 32
> York, county, 333
>> escheators in, 52
> York, dukes of *see* Edmund; Edward
> York (Yorke), Robert, 339

These examples have been deliberately kept simple, but it will be appreciated how essential it is to repeat the words 'Lincoln' and 'York' every time they change their meaning, both because the subentries for the cities and counties are frequently more numerous than most and because they can have sub-subheadings which are only feasible when, for example, 'Lincoln, county,' can be indicated by a single indentation in respect of each of its subentries. Incidentally, there would have been no need to use the word 'diocese' in the first Lincoln entry, if there had been no reference to the diocese as such, but only to the bishop, just as there was no need to insert 'earldom' in the penultimate one because the only references are to earls. The entry would then read

> Lincoln, bishop of *see* Grosseteste,
>> Robert

Before leaving dioceses, we should note that composite ones such as Bath and Wells or Coventry and Lichfield do not precede the other Bath and Coventry entries, but come right at the end, even after any persons named Bath and Coventry. This is in accordance with the word-by-word system of alphabetising recommended below (VII b).

When there are two or more hundreds, towns, parishes or lesser places with the same name or the same significant word, there are three possible ways of arranging their index entries in relation to each other. (They all come after any ecclesiastical area and before any county, as already explained.) One, sometimes recommended, but for good reason rarely put into practice, is to arrange them in descending order of size or importance; but this is far too time-consuming for the indexer and confusing for the user. Another, much more commonly encountered, is for them to be arranged strictly by the alphabetical order of their counties, so that the qualified and unqualified forms of a name are completely mixed, qualifications only influencing the order when there are two or more places with the same main element in the same county. This practice is obviously useful for anyone interested in all places in the same county sharing a significant word, but such persons will be very few and it is not justifiable to break away from a more generally helpful order just for them.

What is here recommended for such places is that those having the homonymous name unqualified should come first, arranged in the alphabetical order of their counties, or equivalent districts if foreign, irrespective of their size and whether or not the county is in square brackets because supplied by the indexer (see III f). But when there are two or more such places in the same county, a hundred comes first, and a town or parish comes before any smaller place. In those rare cases when there are two such parishes in the same county, they should be identified either by reference to the hundreds or wapentakes in which they are situated and arranged in alphabetical order of the hundreds, which should be printed in square brackets, thus

> Newton [in Thriplow hundred], Cambs,
> 426
> Newton [in Wisbech hundred], Cambs,
> 52

but with no cross-references from hundreds to parishes; or, as is more useful in the case of counties which have only a few and very large hundreds, by reference to neighbouring places by which they are traditionally distinguished, thus

> Exhall [near Alcester], Warw, 356
> Exhall [near Coventry], Warw, 187

again in alphabetical order and with no cross-references. Similarly when there are two or more townships or manors with the same name in the same county, they should be alphabetised by their parishes, again irrespective of whether or not they are in square brackets. With the exception of places with identical names, of equal status and in the same county, any descriptions, usually by parishes, included in the index to define a place more exactly should be ignored for purposes of their index order, whether they are supplied by the indexer or named in the text.

After all the simple forms of homonymous place names come those with the same significant word, but qualified. They should be listed according to the alphabetical order of their qualifying words. The fact that some place names will be in their natural order and others will be inverted, with the qualifying word or words separated by a comma, must be disregarded in determining the alphabetical order. So must the fact that some of the words are adjectives and of greater importance than articles and prepositions: alphabetising should be by the first word of the qualification, whatever part of speech it may be, and not by the first significant word. Two runs of such place-name entries might be

> Norton [in Dartmouth], Devon, Row
> of, q.v.
> Norton, Kent, church, 232
> Norton Conyers (Norton, Norton by
> Nunwick) [in Wath], Yorks,
> 345
> Norton Disney, Lincs, Spufford of, q.v.
> Norton in the Moors, Staffs, Stockton
> Brook in, q.v.
> Norton Malreward (Norton Maure-
> ward), Som, 490

Norton sub Hamdon (Norton), Som,
  506
Norton, John, 596
  Richard, 302

Sutton, Suff, Bowen of, *q.v.*
Sutton, Surrey, Oldfields in, *q.v.*
Sutton [in Woking], Surrey, 118
Sutton, King's, (Kynggessutton), Nor-
  thants, hundred, 538
Sutton, King's, (Kynggessutton), Nor-
  thants, manor, 538
Sutton on Hull (Sutton in Holder-
  nesse), Yorks, 365
Sutton Pool (Sutton Pole) [in Plym-
  outh], Devon, 104
Sutton Prior (Sutton Priour) [in Plym-
  outh], Devon, church, 570
Sutton Vautort (Sutton Viutort) in
  Plymouth, Devon, 75, 153
Sutton, John, 181
  Robert, 666

Once again the individual entries have been kept short and simple, but even so
the absolute necessity of repeating the name whenever it starts to represent
another place will be clear. To indent for every new place after the first
would give the impression that the whole long Sutton entry resulting related to
Sutton in Suffolk, as the first six places thus printed immediately below are
sufficient to show

Sutton, Suff, Bowen of, *q.v.*
  Surrey, Oldfields in, *q.v.*
  [in Woking], Surrey, 118
  King's, (Kynggessutton), Northants,
    hundred, 538
    manor, 538
  on Hull (Sutton in Holdernesse),
    Yorks, 365

Some indexers disregard for purposes of alphabetising any words in a heading
which they consider to be of little significance, so that the entries after Norton
Disney would follow in the order

Norton sub Hamdon (Norton), Som,
  506
Norton Malreward (Norton Maure-
  ward), Som, 490
Norton in the Moors, Staffs, Stockton
  Brook in, *q.v.*

and in the second example Sutton on Hull would precede King's Sutton hundred.
Although words such as 'sub', 'on the', 'by' and 'juxta' are less important than
the words they link, they are by no means unimportant; and the easier and more
natural practice is to alphabetise by each successive word in turn irrespective
of its significance. The same applies to subject headings, although with them it

is a problem which is rarely encountered in Subject Indexes to record publications; and to their subentries (see V g). Those who ignore articles, conjunctions and prepositions in determining alphabetical order often feel obliged to indicate that fact in one of two ways: either by differentiating the words ignored typographically, which serves only to give them added emphasis rather than less; or by enclosing them in round brackets, which not only looks ungainly but is impossible for place names because of the use of brackets for other purposes, especially to enclose obsolete forms. It is therefore recommended that for determining alphabetical order all words in the same relative position in headings should carry equal weight.

(o) *Foreign Places*
The main principles stated above apply to foreign place names. They should be identified and indexed under their most modern spellings, which are to be found in the most recent standard atlases and gazetteers.[8] When there is a recognised English form it should be used rather than the foreign one: for example, Brussels and Cologne, not Bruxelles and Köln. But places which have undergone a complete change of name or which vary markedly in form from time to time according to which side of a fluctuating frontier they happen to lie on, like Aix la Chapelle *alias* Aachen, should be indexed under the modernised form of the name used at the time of the compilation of the documents, which will be that used in the text, with a simple cross-reference from the other if the name in the documents is not the present-day one. It is recommended that such entries should take the form

> Danzig, Prussia, (*now* Gdansk, prov.
> Gdansk, Poland), 531
> Gdansk *see* Danzig

This is, of course, a problem with which one is seldom confronted in dealing with British places. Some have completely changed their names, Meeching to Newhaven and Gingeyberdlaundry to Buttsbury, but such changes usually took place at a fairly early date and the earlier names can be treated exactly as if they were normal obsolete forms, except that they should always be given italicised in brackets after the modern forms in the text of calendars and descriptive lists.

Just as British places are indexed with reference to parish and county, so should foreign places be given a corresponding identification by whatever geographical areas are appropriate to the country concerned and also by the country itself. Except for very small places, it is usually sufficient to give merely the department for France, the province for Holland and Spain, and so on, as in these examples

> Calais, [dep. Pas de Calais], France, 62
> Caen (*Cadamo*), [dep. Calvados,
> France], abbess of, 183
> Zierikzee (Selissay, Selykey), [prov.
> Zeeland, Holland], 222
> Corunna (le Groyne), [prov. Corunna,
> Spain], 356

Corunna is, of course, the English form and is to be preferred in English indexes to the Spanish Coruña.

[8] The best general ones are probably *The Times Atlas of the World*, 5 vols (1955-9) and *The Times Index-Gazetteer of the World* (1965).

European places with simple prefixes, such as Le Havre, Le Mans and La Rochelle, must be inverted for indexing: for example

> Rochelle, La, (la Rochell, *Rupella*),
>   [dep. Charente Maritime],
> France, 201

in order to avoid what might sometimes amount to many pages of entries beginning with every article. But this rule does not apply to the similar and less numerous places in the New World. Thus Des Moines, Iowa, is indexed under 'D' and is alphabetised as if it were spelt as a single word, as is explained more fully in connection with prefixed surnames (IV g).

In modern records some countries are described by their full titles, the first word of which may be merely descriptive of political status. Two examples are the Commonwealth of Australia and the Union of South Africa. They should be indexed under Australia and South Africa, although cross-references can be given from the full titles. But an exception can be made for the United States of America, which should be indexed under 'U', with a cross-reference from America, because that country is so frequently called 'the United States'.

The rules for inverting, which are applied uniformly to British place names, should be ignored for most Commonwealth and ex-Commonwealth countries and the Americas: for the names of the countries themselves and for places within them. It would be unthinkable to index New Zealand, New South Wales, New Guinea, New Brunswick, New York, New Orleans, Nova Scotia, West Indies and East Indies under anything but New, Nova, West and East. These first words, although adjectival, are always thought of as much more vital parts of the names and the second ones as correspondingly less important than in equivalent British place names. New York, for example, would never be referred to locally as York, unlike Bishop's Stortford and Stanton St John which local people commonly abbreviate to Stortford and Stanton. Part of the explanation must lie in the fact that the qualifying element of the Commonwealth and American names is frequently to distinguish them from (or perhaps rather to associate them with) the corresponding unqualified places in a different part of the world, usually the Old World, although the Carolinas should also be indexed under North and South.

Finally, in many volumes devoted to British records there will be only a few index entries relating to foreign places. In such cases it is helpful to repeat them under the headings of the relevant countries. The two entries

> Bordeaux, [dep. Gironde], France,
>   ship *la Marie* of, 134
> Rochelle, La, (la Rochell), [dep. Char-
>   ente Maritime], France, ship
>   *Notre Dame* of, 552

warrant a third

>   France, ships of, 134, 552

to save searchers interested in that country from having to go all through the index or the text for a few chance references. What should not be done, but occasionally is, is to put all the French places as subheadings under the heading 'France' without also having them in their correct alphabetical positions in the index. Whereas their inclusion twice—in their correct positions and under France—can be justified if space is no consideration, when, as is usual, they can be entered only once it must be in their own right where they would first be looked for.

CHAPTER IV

PERSONS

(a) *What Persons to Index*

Just as every place mentioned in the text of a record publication in its own right requires an entry or subentry in the index, with one reference for each separate occurrence, so does every person. To this general rule the inevitable exceptions are few, minor and fairly obvious. In the same way as counties are never indexed when they are mentioned not for their own sake but merely to identify places, so monarchs, popes and bishops can be ignored when they occur for dating purposes and not as persons.[1] Equally, when the monarch, whether named or described as 'the king', is used as a synonym for 'the crown', in other words when the institution rather than the person is denoted, no entry is required in the Index of Persons, although it may be both legitimate and desirable to have one in the Subject Index, even under the king's name. It may sound strange to recommend that kings be treated as subjects, but in many cases that is what they are in the text. When they are mentioned as persons, however, they must be entered in the Index of Persons and Places. Clearly cross-references between the two indexes will often be useful.

There are other mentions of persons which do not require indexing as such. 'The French' should never be indexed as

French, the, 76

and rarely as

France, men of, 76

The context usually reads 'the war against the French', or something similar, and the index entry should then be

France, war with, 76

Specific surnames are sometimes used to describe a subject, in which case they should appear only in the Subject Index. Parkinson's disease no more warrants an entry under the surname Parkinson than does the French pox under France. Both should be in the Subject Index, probably under the heading 'Diseases'. Similarly, the *Curia Regis Rolls* have entries relating to Bracton's Note Book in their Subject Indexes, although references to Bracton himself, whether as a justice or as a private individual, are under his name in the Index of Persons and Places.

Other personal names which need not, and should not, be indexed are those which are largely missing because of a defective manuscript and cannot be guessed. Neither persons nor places are worth indexing if only an initial letter or one or two in the middle of the name can be read because the document is faded, stained, decayed or torn. To have index entries reading

R . . . , 74

. . . cr . . . , 88

is to waste space, whether they are put at the very end of the index or in the

---

[1] 'In the year 5 Charles I' is clearly a date. So normally is 'in the time of King John', but in some contexts such phrases have connotations additional to the temporal one. Thus King John can justifiably be indexed as a person in the passage: 'This was the worst example of monarchical tyranny since the time of King John'.

alphabetical positions required by their surviving letters. The latter practice is, of course, particularly futile when the initial letter is missing. It is also not worth indexing persons known only by their forenames because their surnames are illegible or were inadvertently omitted from the original record, unless they are described as holding an office or benefice when they should be indexed under the relevant place (see IV m). Very few searchers would either look up or follow up such entries as

John ... , 29

on the chance that the person in whom they were interested occurred merely by his forename.

On the other hand, persons who occur in the text without a forename and whose forenames cannot be discovered are worth indexing. They should come before all the other people with the same surname, as in this example

Goddard, ... , 76

Alan, 239

John, 54

Richard, 792

Robert, 299

Sometimes there is a strong probability that the man without the forename is the same as one of the others, in which case the following index entries are recommended

Brown, Captain ... [?Robert], 52

John, 726

Matthew, 594

Captain Robert, 3, ?52, 663

People whose forenames do not occur in the text but can be discovered from other sources should be indexed with their forenames in their correct alphabetical order but in square brackets. There may also be people whose forenames are represented by initials. When they can be readily discovered, they should be indexed with their forenames spelled out. Otherwise they can only be indexed with the initials representing the forenames, before other people with the same surname and initials but whose forenames are known (see IV k).

Persons who occur in the text wholly in the form of initials, often as signatories of letters, should also be indexed. If their names can be discovered they must be indexed under them, with cross-references from the initials. The cross-references should be both from the order in which the initials occur in the text and also from the inverted order, with the last first, as users of the text might look up either. The initials should also be given in brackets after the whole name, to warn the searcher who turns first to the name that he may well find only initials in the text. Typical index entries might therefore read

Brown, Matthew, (M.B.), 56, 72, 594

M.B. *see* Brown, Matthew

B., M. *see* Brown, Matthew

Sometimes, however, it is impossible to identify such people, possibly because the letters are not genuine initials but are a code name. In that case they should be indexed by the letters alone, and, because they may or may not represent forename, or forenames, and surname, it is as well to include them in the text order and inverted, for example

A.B.C., 40

C., A.B., 40

Some may question the value of indexing the names of people whose occurrence in a volume could not conceivably be anticipated. For example, few people would expect to find King Athelstan in the index to fifteenth-century documents. But if a Chancery enrolment of that date refers to a grant of lands or privileges made by him, he must be indexed as a person. Nobody can say that a persevering searcher will never look for Athelstan in an index to fifteenth-century records. He may, indeed, have excellent reasons for expecting to find him or equally unlikely people (and places) there.

(b) *Standardisation of Surnames*

Personal names have not been indexed as consistently as place names. Many of the better indexers make no attempt to modernise or standardise them, with the result that the same persons can be found indexed under a different form in every volume in which they appear, even in successive volumes of the same series. The normal practice of the better indexers today is to translate Latin surnames into the modern English equivalent and to index the others, the vast majority even in early documents, under whatever forms used in the manuscripts most closely approximate to the most common of the corresponding modern surnames. The other forms found in the manuscripts are given, preferably in brackets, after the chosen forms, with cross-references from them to the chosen forms unless they would be adjacent in the index. All persons sharing a surname, whether they are related or not, are given as subentries of the surname in alphabetical order. Thus a simple entry might read

> Marshe (Mareis, Mareys, *Marisco*,
> Mershe, Mersshe), Henry atte,
> 32
> John de, 77
> Richard, 39
> Robert ate, 339
> Walter de, 524
> William atte, 707

This entry, in which Mareis and Mareys are French forms and *Marisco* is italicised because it is in Latin,[2] would probably require a separate cross-reference from each version in brackets, in the form

> Mareis *see* Marshe
> Mareys *see* Marshe
> *Marisco see* Marshe

and so on, although in some indexes the last two forms might be adjacent and so could be combined to give the entry

> Mershe, Mersshe *see* Marshe

If nobody had been called Marshe, the name chosen for the main entry would have been Mershe, which is the next most modern, or least aberrant.

When an uncommon name occurs only once in the text it may be in a grotesque spelling. Nevertheless, the consistent application of the system just described demands that it shall be the sole form of it to be found in the index. This results at best in a tedious search when anybody wishes to discover a particular person or family in a number of volumes, and he will rarely be certain that he has

---

[2] *Marisco* is in the ablative because it is governed by the 'de' of 'Walter de'. This use of italics is far from general, but it is recommended here because it is useful to see at a glance which are Latin and which vernacular forms.

secured every reference. It also frequently results in a deliberate, and infuriating, separation, sometimes amounting to pages, of a modernised place name from the surname derived from it, which is indexed under the least bizarre of its manuscript forms. Thus on one page there might be the entry

> Shurnock (Schyrnak, Shernak) [in
> Feckenham], Worcs, manor,
> 359

on another

> Shernak (Schyrnak), John, 359
> Shernak *see* Shurnock

and on a third

> Schyrnak *see* Shernak; Shurnock

This is a typical example in that the references under the person and the place are often the same, and the manuscript forms are frequently identical.

Because of such inconsistencies much thought has recently been given to the possibility of indexing surnames, or at least those which have well defined modern forms, under a standard modern spelling, whether or not that spelling appears in the text. Mr R. E. Latham has suggested the following rules for standardising surnames.

(i) Surnames derived from occupations should be indexed, where practicable, under the standard modern form of the corresponding noun. Thus Tailor would be preferred to Taylor, even though the latter is now the commonest form of the surname; and Smith would embrace not only Smyth and Smythe, but also Faber and le Fevre where the bearer is English or resident in England.

(ii) The like rule should apply to descriptive surnames, bringing Niger, le Neyr and Blak together under Black, and Juvenis, le Joefne and Yong under Young; and to surnames derived from local features, de Ponte and atte Brigge being indexed under Bridge.

(iii) Patronymics appearing in Latin should continue to be indexed as at present under the name of the father modernised in accordance with the normal rules for Christian names. Thus *Hugo filius Johannis* would become 'John, Hugh son of'. If the same man appears elsewhere in the volume in such forms as le filz Jehan or Jonesson, there can be no objection to grouping all the entries under John; but where it is not clear whether these forms represent patronymics in the literal sense, it is safer to index them separately, but it is then generally desirable in medieval volumes to add a cross-reference from John. Christian names used as surnames should be modernised: Baudewyn to Baldwin, Rainald to Reynold, and so on.

(iv) Surnames derived from clearly recognizable British place names should be indexed under the modern forms, but without necessarily attempting a precise identification. Thus Neueton and Niweton would be under Newton, but with no attempt to distinguish between the various places so called. Surnames that may refer to two or more distinct place-name forms, such as Eston to Aston or Easton and Kyrkeby to Kirby or Kirkby, should be grouped together under one of these, normally the one to which the documentary form most closely approximates (Easton and Kirkby in the examples cited). But if in a particular index the surname Eston appears only as the name of a man known to come from an Aston, there can be no objection to indexing him under Aston with a cross-reference from Easton.

This rule cannot be rigidly applied to English surnames derived from foreign, especially French, place names, whose modern names may be obscure and unfamiliar and widely different from any surname ever current in England. Many of these are names that have become firmly established among the English gentry in a standardised form (for example Beauchamp, Darcy and Devereux) that is likely to be familiar both to indexer and user and which should therefore be adopted even if it was not a form current at the date of the document.

(v) There will remain a residue of surnames that cannot readily be standardised on any general principle. Here it will be up to the indexer to ensure continuity within any given series of volumes and also to select normal rather than aberrant forms by reference to such publications as *The Book of Fees* and the *Calendar of Inquisitions Post Mortem*.

There are several possible objections to Mr Latham's scheme. The most general is that while it might have had much to commend it if it had been introduced a century or so ago and been applied to all subsequent record publications, there is much less justification for suddenly introducing it now, after so much has been published with indexes compiled on different lines. Against this objection it can be argued that it is impossible to visualise the day when record publication will cease, and that the records published so far will ultimately form a (thereafter decreasing) minority of those in print. Moreover, Mr Latham does not just advocate the substitution of one indexing system for another, but the introduction for the first time of a high degree of standardisation in the indexing of surnames, which has inherent value however late in the day it is introduced.

It may be more tellingly objected that Mr Latham's scheme has arisen out of the problems which confront the indexer of early records, and that he may have been slightly misled by the analogy of place names, which can be indexed according to unvarying rules irrespective of the period of the documents, into assuming that the same is true of surnames. In fact, the treatment of surnames must vary according to period, and it is here recommended that they be indexed in the following ways according to which of the three periods listed the records derive from.

(i) The Middle Ages, to *c.* 1500. This is the period for which the Latham rules can be applied most completely, with any modifications mentioned later in this section and the next. There must be as many cross-references as are necessary from the manuscript forms of each surname to the standard form, and all the manuscript forms must be printed after the standard form, in brackets and in alphabetical order, as with obsolete forms of place names.

(ii) The early modern period, *c.* 1500-1750. The Latham rules can be similarly applied to documents of this date, except that completely different words should no longer be brought together. Thus whereas for medieval volumes it is perfectly legitimate to index Faber and le Fevre under Smith, after 1500 they should be kept separate because they may all be regarded as different English names, if applied to Englishmen, and not as Latin, French and English versions of the same name. Only the different spellings of Smith—Smyth, Smythe, etc.—should be brought together under that name, although 'see also' or 'cf.' cross-references between Smith, Faber and Le Fevre are advisable for the sixteenth century. Because the variations between the standard form and the manuscript ones will normally be very slight by this date, the manuscripts having a 'y' for an 'i', one 'n' instead of two, and so on, there need be cross-references in the index from the manuscript to the standard forms only for those few names which are not immediately recognizable or which start with a different initial letter, for instance a 'C' in place of a 'K'. Indeed, if space is very short, the unexceptional obsolete or variant forms need not even be given in brackets after the standard one, since the variations should be sufficiently slight for the name to be immediately recognizable in the text from the standard form.

(iii) The late modern period, from c. 1750. It is difficult to see how the Latham proposals could be usefully applied to most administrative records of this period.[3] Since 1750 most families and individuals have come to be known under a single fixed spelling of their surnames, which is the spelling normally found in modern records and under which searchers would rightly expect to find them indexed. Any minor variations can be dealt with by simple cross-references. As will be seen later in this chapter, the indexing of modern surnames has many difficulties, but the need to standardise is not one of them. There would be more loss than gain and it would be more frustrating than helpful if such indexes were compiled according to the Latham rules.

It is important to note that the manuscript and not the standardised forms of surnames should always be used in the text of calendars and descriptive lists, despite the fact that it is recommended that the modern spellings of place names should be used in such texts after 1400 (see III d). To substitute the standard forms would tend to suggest that they were the forms into which the obsolete ones developed, which would often be untrue. Mr Latham does not advocate 'identifying' surnames in the way in which places are identified. That would be impossible in most cases. Whereas every place has a single modern spelling, there are a number of different modern spellings or forms of many individual early surnames, some of which are now more commonly found than the standardised ones resulting from the Latham rules. The standardised spellings are merely intended to make the indexes more easily usable. With cross-references from the manuscript forms in medieval volumes, nobody would be worse off than with the more traditional indexes and many would be saved much time.

Three cautionary notes must be sounded before we leave this topic. First, up to ten per cent of surnames in many volumes will prove unamenable to standardisation and must be indexed in their manuscript forms. Secondly, there are certain historical figures who have become well known by rather eccentric spellings: names which would not normally appear in Latham indexes except as cross-references. Two such are William of Wykeham and Bartholomew Burghersh. By the strict letter of the Latham rules they should be indexed under Wickham and Burwash. Unseemly as it will appear to Wykehamists, that is justifiable and is here recommended, provided that cross-references are given from Wykeham and Burghersh whether or not these forms appear in the text. The alternatives—to index William under Wykeham and all the other Wickhams under Wickham with 'see also' cross-references between them, or to have all the Wickhams under Wykeham—have their attractions in this case, but once general rules are breached it becomes ever more difficult to apply them at other points. It is on these grounds that Mr Latham suggests Tailor rather than Taylor as the standard form, although there should again always be a cross-reference from

[3] There are exceptions, and Mr M. Roper tells me that the 19th-century Census Returns are among them. Because the names were written to accord with their sound when spoken by their often illiterate owners, the spellings are only approximately correct and therefore suitable for standardisation.

Taylor, whether or not that form occurs in the text, because it is by such a wide margin the most common spelling of the surname today.

Thirdly, whereas it is fairly easy to decide upon standard forms of patronymics and occupational surnames, those derived from place names can present great difficulties. A considerable knowledge of local place names and families is often necessary before it can be confidently decided whether to call a person Stratton or Stretton; and when the family or individual is obscure and there are a number of similar places close together which shared common obsolete forms, even the local expert can be beaten. The difficulties confronting an indexer of records covering the whole country are far greater. In one index[4] compiled according to the Latham rules slightly modified, it was impossible to distinguish between people whose names derived from Haughton, Hawton, Houghton and Hutton. That was because, while the first two can hardly be confused with the last, Haughton and Hawton naturally share obsolete forms, as do Haughton and Houghton, while Houghton and Hutton share such forms as Hoton, and all these overlapping forms occurred in the text. The solution adopted was to bring all the people together into a single composite entry under the heading

Haughton, Hawton, Houghton and
Hutton

with cross-references from the last three names to the first. This is an extreme example, but it may often be necessary, especially for records of the early modern period, to have composite entries for such pairs of names as Black and Blake, Peck and Peak, and Stocks and Stokes, when it is impossible to disentangle obscure families or when there is doubt in respect of a single person or family. There must, of course, always be a cross-reference from the second name to the first unless they are alphabetically adjacent.

(c) *Early Names: Patronymics*
It will be remembered that in his third rule (IV b) Mr Latham recommended that *Hugo filius Johannis* should be indexed as

John, Hugh son of, 229

and not as

Hugh son of John, 229

as is the practice in some indexes to early medieval records. The former is to be preferred, because while there is always a chance that Hugh and his descendants came to be known as Johns, Johnson or some such name, it is much less likely that the forename Hugh formed the basis of their ultimate surname. Moreover, before 1300 other kinds of names were often no more settled than patronymics. *Johannes Piscator* may often be John the fisherman, his occupation, rather than John Fisher, although he could be both; and John le Rede may genuinely have been a red-headed man whose black-haired son was given a different nickname. Thus the logical result of indexing Hugh son of John under Hugh would be to index everyone under his forename, as the French do in their editions of medieval documents. That not only results in many pages of similar entries, since medieval forenames, especially those of men, lacked variety, but also hides the genuine surnames. The French cross-refer from surnames to forenames, but that wastes much space. It is therefore recommended that, with the exception of special groups of people dealt with below (IV j, p, q), forenames should always come

---

[4] *Calendar of Nottinghamshire Coroners' Inquests, 1485-1558*, ed. R. F. Hunnisett (Thoroton Soc. Rec. Ser., xxv).

second in index entries. This is the more satisfactory practice and it in no way commits the indexer to a decision as to whether or not the other part of the name is a genuine surname.

Hugo filius Johannis will, of course, appear as such in a full transcript of a Latin document, but will be translated as Hugh son of John in a calendar or descriptive list. In neither case need the Latin form appear in the index. Latin forenames should always be indexed under their normal English rendering, as given in works such as *The Record Interpreter*.[5] But it is useful for the Latin forms of occupational names and descriptive nicknames, for example *Piscator* and *Niger*, to be preserved in the text of calendars and lists and as cross-references in the index, although the main entries would be under the normal English translation

> Fisher (*Piscator*), Robert, 334
> Black (*Niger*), John, 592

Once again, the English equivalents of the most common Latin surnames will be found in *The Record Interpreter*.

In documents written in French, and also in some Latin ones, Hugh son of John will appear in some such form as Hugh le filz Jehan. Once again this must be left as it is in a calendar or list, but it is recommended that it be indexed as follows

> Jehan *see* John
> John (Jehan), Hugh le filz, 76

If he appears elsewhere in the same volume as *Hugo filius Johannis*, or translated into English for a calendar or list, the main entry should read

> John (Jehan), Hugh son of *alias* Hugh
> le filz, 76, 89

The temptation, particularly strong in the case of the French version, to index him as Fitz John should be resisted, unless there is conclusive proof that this really was or became his family name. Such families are few, but when they occur, in whatever form, they should be indexed under Fitz. Thus if *Ricardus filius Alani* is definitely known to have been a member of the famous Fitz Alan family, he must be indexed as

> Fitz Alan, Richard, 992

with the cross-reference

> Alan *see* Fitz Alan

or, if there are other Alans,

> Alan, John son of, 22
> William, 354
> *See also* Fitz Alan

For arranging in alphabetical order, surnames beginning with Fitz should be treated as if spelt as a single word, Fitz William coming after Fitzgibbon.

Our Hugh may appear in the manuscripts as *Hugo filius Johannis de Langele*. The indexer of records later than 1300 is justified in regarding him as Hugh the son of a man named John de Langley and should index him accordingly. But in earlier documents he may equally well be Hugh son of John and living in one

---

[5] C. T. Martin, *The Record Interpreter*, 2nd edn (1910). This should be used in conjunction with E. G. Withycombe, *The Oxford Dictionary of English Christian Names* (Oxford, 1945).

of the Langleys. Such ambiguously described persons in very early documents should therefore be indexed twice as

> Langley (Langele), John de, Hugh son
> of, *or* Hugh son of John of
> ?King's Langley, 156
> John, Hugh son of, of ?King's Lang-
> ley, *or* Hugh son of John de
> Langley (Langele), 156

with the cross-references

> Langele *see* Langley
> Langley, ?King's, (Langele), Herts,
> John of, *q.v.*

It is assumed in this example that there is a strong probability, but not conclusive proof, that Langley is King's Langley, as is indicated according to the rule already given (III g). There will often be similar uncertainty in pre-1300 records with words which may be either occupations or occupational surnames. Thus *Ricardus filius Willelmi Faber* could be either a smith named Richard son of William (a smith would certainly not have been named Fitz William) or the son of a man named William Smith. His index entries would accordingly read

> Smith (*Faber*), William, Richard son
> of, *or* Richard son of William,
> smith, 18
> William, Richard son of, smith, *or*
> Richard son of William Smith,
> 18
> *Faber see* Smith

The word '*or*' is used instead of '*alias*' because it separates two possible interpretations of a single form of a name, whereas '*alias*' is reserved for alternative forms both of which appear in the text (see IV e).

(d) *Early Names: Servants*

Walter Jonesservant le Marshall is a form of name occasionally encountered throughout the Middle Ages, in which a servant's or official's title unites his name with that of his master or a place. The servant is not Walter Jones, but Walter the servant of John le Marshall. He should therefore be indexed as

> Marshal (Marshall), John le, Walter
> servant of (Walter Jonesservant
> le Marshall), 654

The manuscript form is worth a place in brackets for ease of recognition in the text, but there is no need to have a second entry, even by way of cross-reference, under Walter. Nobody would look for such an obscure person under a common forename. Only if the name is given as Walter Smith Jonesservant le Marshall should there be two entries, one under Smith and one under Marshal, according to the rules for indexing officials and servants given below (IV m).

Even more infrequently relationships are found similarly incorporated within names, for example Alice Wyllsdoghtre de Clympyng. She would likewise be indexed as

> Climping (Clympyng), William de,
> Alice daughter of (Alice Wylls-
> doghtre de Clympyng), 6

(e) *Early Names: the Use of* alias

In the early Middle Ages, before surnames had fully evolved, one man might be described in terms of his father, his occupation and a place, or even by a descriptive nickname, at different points in the same volume. Sometimes it becomes apparent to the editor or indexer that these are different descriptions of the same man, in which case that fact must be made obvious in the index. This can be done in any of three ways. One, which is not recommended for reasons already given (IV c), is to adopt the French practice of having the main entry under the forename, with cross-references from all the second names. The other practices are better. The first is to adopt one description as the main entry under which to give all the references, merely cross-referring from the others, as follows

> John, Hugh son of *see* Langley
> Butcher (Bocher) *see* Langley
> Langley (Langele), Hugh de, *alias*
>   Hugh Butcher (Bocher) *alias*
>   Hugh son of John, 78, 145, 252

The manuscript form of Butcher is supplied under Langley for ease of recognition in the text. There must also, of course, be two other cross-references, one being

> Langele *see* Langley

and the other either

> Bocher *see* Butcher

if there are other Bochers, or

> Bocher *see* Langley

which would be a kindness to the searcher if Hugh were the only Bocher.

Alternatively, the references and all descriptions could be given three times thus

> Butcher (Bocher), Hugh, *alias* Hugh
>   de Langley (Langele) *alias*
>   Hugh son of John, 78, 145, 252
> John, Hugh son of, *alias* Hugh Butcher
>   (Bocher) *alias* Hugh de Langley
>   (Langele), 78, 145, 252
> Langley (Langele), Hugh de, *alias*
>   Hugh Butcher (Bocher) *alias*
>   Hugh son of John, 78, 145, 252

with the usual cross-references from Bocher and Langele. In neither case are cross-references required from Hugh.

It will be noticed that in the first of our preferred practices, which will often be the one used because it takes up less space, all the references are given under just one of the forms, while in the second, which is recommended if space is plentiful, they are all given under all of them. They should never be split up, with some under one and some under another according to the manuscript forms to be found by the particular references, even if two-way, or in our example three-way, cross-references are provided.

The entries containing a person described in utterly different ways will often be more complex than in the preceding examples. Such persons will often form subentries, as here

> John, Adam son of, 54
>   Edward son of, 67

> John (*contd*)
>> Hugh son of, *alias* Hugh Butcher
>> (Bocher) *alias* Hugh de Langley
>> (Langele), 78, 145, 252
>> Matthew son of, 38, 367
> Butcher (Bocher), Bertram, 62
> Henry, 533
> Hugh, *alias* Hugh de Langley
> (Langele) *alias* Hugh son of
> John, 78, 145, 252
> Richard, 233

and similarly with Langley. No other usage is quite as explicit and the user will appreciate that in such a context the word *alias* does not appear in the text of early records and that the different forms occur at different points.

From the thirteenth century onwards, however, and not only in the Middle Ages, many people, particularly felons, are described by two or more alternative names, linked by the word *alias*, in the same line of a document, and they can be indexed similarly: either with the reference given only once, as in

> Bluebeard (Bleuberd) *see* Johnson
> Johnson (Jonesson) *alias* Bluebeard,
>> Andrew, 76

or, as is preferable, under each form, as follows

> Bluebeard (Bleuberd) *alias* Johnson,
>> Andrew, 76
> Johnson (Jonesson) *alias* Bluebeard,
>> Andrew, 76

Once again, care must be taken when there are a number of different Johnsons, or indeed Bluebeards, to ensure that the *alias* is associated with the correct man and with him alone. The following entry is wrong, because imprecise

> Johnson (Jonesson, Jonsson) *alias*
>> Bluebeard, Agnes, 342
>> Amy, 543
>> Andrew, 76
>> Bartholomew, 188

Bluebeard being not an alternative name which any of the Johnsons might have used, like the obsolete forms of Johnson, but a different name deliberately adopted by, or applied to, just one of them. The correct reading would therefore be

> Johnson (Jonesson, Jonsson), Agnes,
>> 342
>> Amy, 543
>> Andrew, *alias* Andrew Bluebeard,
>> 76
>> Bartholomew, 188

Some indexers put the straight Johnsons first, in alphabetical order of forenames, followed by the separate entry

> Johnson *alias* Bluebeard, Andrew, 76

This practice is not recommended because a searcher might look for Andrew Johnson unaware of his *alias*. Having failed to find him in his correct alphabetical position among the Johnsons, he would naturally not look further, his eye might not chance upon the next entry and so he would miss his reference.

In some records, particularly those of the Tudor period, variant forms of names are given with *aliases*: for example, Andrew Jonesson *alias* Andrew Jonnson *alias* Andrew Jonsson. These need only be indexed in the normal way, namely

Johnson (Jonesson, Jonnson, Jonsson),
Andrew, 76

In yet later records persons may be mentioned under their true names who are far better known by pseudonyms. They can usefully be indexed twice, in the form

Evans, Mary Ann, [*alias* George Eliot],
316
Eliot, George, *alias* Mary Ann Evans,
316

or, alternatively, with a cross-reference from 'Eliot, George', not just from 'Eliot'. The *alias* in the Evans entry is in square brackets because the information is supplied by the indexer from sources outside the text.

To return to early documents, in the Middle Ages the same person may occur sometimes as Hugh Langele and sometimes as Hugh de Langele. He will often be found indexed in this way

Langley (Langele), Hugh (de), 79, 122,
145, 633

There are two reasons for discouraging such a use of round brackets. One is because they have been recommended for the enclosure of obsolete forms of personal and place names. Their use around 'de' might therefore suggest not that that word sometimes occurs and sometimes does not, but that it always occurs and has been virtually removed from the index for reasons of modernisation. This is the same argument as was used (III c) to discourage the similar use of round brackets to indicate that the adjectival part of a place name sometimes appears in the text, but not always. Secondly, brackets cannot be used when the same man is called both Hugh atte Mershe and Hugh du Mareis. He must be indexed as

Marsh (Mareis, Mershe), Hugh atte
alias Hugh du, 29, 177

Therefore, in the interests of consistency, it is best to use *alias* in all such cases, although it may make such entries slightly longer; and so our Langley entry should read

Langley (Langele), Hugh *alias* Hugh
de, 79, 122, 145, 633

Alias should also be used on those rare occasions when two separate forenames are deliberately adopted by or assigned to a single individual. But when the same man is erroneously called, for example, John at one point in the text and William at another and there is no doubt that one and the same person is meant, but it is impossible to know which name was the correct one, he should be indexed as

Marsh, John *or* William, 22

or, if there are others with the same surname who would normally be placed between the two forenames if they belonged to different people, he must be indexed twice as follows

Marsh, Andrew, 78
John *or* William, 22
Richard, 674
Robert, 299
William *or* John, 22

This is necessary because his true name might have been either John or William, and any searcher knowing which it was and having no reason to suspect that he might appear with a different forename would have a fifty-fifty chance of missing him if, in a hurry, he merely looked for the correct name when only one of the above subentries had been included. Moreover, the inclusion of only one of them implies that the indexer had reason to believe that the name mentioned first, by which the man is alphabetised, was the true one. When he has such knowledge, which is quite often since the wrong name frequently occurs only once as against several occurrences of the correct one or, alternatively, because one name is clearly a scribal error ('the said William Marsh', when John Marsh had recently been mentioned), the index entry should read

> Marsh, John (*once called* William), 22,
>   99, 108
> Richard, 674
> Robert, 299
> William (*recte* John), 22, 99, 108

or, in place of the last line,

> William *see* John

(f) *Early Names: Prefixes*

It will have been noticed that in the foregoing examples no attempt has been made to translate or modernise articles and prepositions forming part of early personal names: 'atte' to 'at', 'de' to 'of', 'de la' and 'du' to 'of the', and 'le', 'la' and 'les' to 'the'. This has been done in a few indexes, but it is not recommended here, despite the earlier recommendation (IV b) that surnames proper be modernised, because such words mostly dropped out. Only a few people, like William of Wykeham, are today commonly known with the article or preposition retained and modernised or translated. A few names ultimately had the prefix attached to the main part, as in Atwell, while in a few others it survived in its original form as a separate word. The treatment of such words, when they occur in later documents, will be discussed in the next section. This section is concerned only with the Middle Ages, and it is useful for students of early personal names for the prefixes to be given in the index in their manuscript forms. They should always follow the forenames and never precede the surnames, otherwise the index would be overweighted with names beginning 'de', 'le' and so on. It is not even necessary to have omnibus cross-references such as

> de. *For names preceded by this word see*
>   *the main element*

But when the article and/or preposition and the main surname are written in the manuscript as a single word, a cross-reference is necessary, for example

> Lestrange *see* Strange
> Strange (*Extraneus*, Lestrange), John
>   *alias* John le, 27, 89, 156

The searcher will realise that the entry containing 'John le' has the surname Strange, whereas the other two forms are preceded by the simple John. Another series of entries might similarly be

> Atwelle *see* Well
> Well (Atwelle, *Fonte*, *Fontem*, Welle),
>   John atte, 66
>   Richard *alias* Richard *ad*, 155, 276

Well (*contd*)
    Robert ate, 92
    William atte *alias* William de, 276,
        594

For post-1500 documents, however, Lestrange and Atwell should be indexed as separate names, although with two-way '*see also*' or '*cf.*' cross-references with Strange and Well. By that date the Latin forms will have dropped out.

(g) *Modern Prefixes, English and Foreign*

After 1500 prefixes became an integral part of a few English and American surnames, and when such names occur in post-medieval documents they should be indexed by their prefixes. Thus De La Warr, De La Mare and De Quincey will all come under 'D', although in early modern records it is as well to have a cross-reference from the final word. Moreover, whatever system of alphabetising is used (see VII b), such names should be treated as if they were spelt as single words, so that a series of entries might run

    Debenham, Suff, 220
    De La Mare, Walter, 55, 316
    De La Warr, Edward, 67
    Denham, Bucks, 522
    De Quincey, John, 326

The justification for this treatment is that the prefixes are integral parts of the name, are hardly separate words and are never thought of as such: they have no significance out of their context. Indeed, it is pure chance that some prefixes are still separate, while others have been joined to the main name to form a single word such as Atwood and Attlee.

For post-medieval foreign names with prefixes the rule is slightly more complex. In the index articles, and compounds of articles and prepositions, precede the main part of the name, but the main name comes first and the prefix follows all forenames if the prefix is a preposition. Thus French names beginning with 'L'', 'Le', 'La', 'Les', 'Du' and 'Des' are indexed under those words and are alphabetised in the same way as English and American names with prefixes, La Fontaine always coming after Labrador. The same applies to Italian and Spanish names beginning 'La' and 'Lo', 'Dal', 'Del' and 'Della'. But names with 'D'', 'De', 'Da', 'Von' and 'Van' should be indexed, like medieval names, under the word following, because such prefixes are not regarded as integral parts of the name; and the prefixes themselves should be inverted to follow the forenames. Thus Van Gogh should be indexed as

    Gogh, Vincent Willem Van, 394

and the Nazi minister as

    Ribbentrop, Joachim von, 56

although, because the former is popularly known as Van Gogh, it would be considerate to have the cross-reference

    Van Gogh *see* Gogh

or, if there were several such names, the more general cross-reference

    Van. *For names with this prefix see the*
        main element

Van Dyck, however, was so closely associated with England that it is justifiable to treat him as though he were English, indexing him as

    Van Dyck, Sir Anthony, 776

but with the cross-reference

Dyck see Van Dyck

Where prefixes have been joined with the rest of the name to form a single word, for example Vandervelde, there can, of course, be no question of separating them for indexing purposes and the name must be indexed straightforwardly, primarily under what was the prefix.

(h) *Compound Surnames*

Strictly, the rule for indexing compound, or double-barrelled, surnames is to index under the first word and cross-refer from the second. It can be safely applied to all foreign names, but many English names which at first sight appear to be compound ones do not consist of two genuine surnames. Most hyphenated names are genuine, as are some without hyphens, and the rule can be applied to them. But in many other cases only the final name is a surname. This is usually true of Welshmen who use a forename with their surname to distinguish themselves from others with the same surname. Thus Arthur Tudor Williams and Margaret Lloyd Jones should be indexed as

Williams, Arthur Tudor, 31
Jones, Margaret Lloyd, 54

although they may have been called Mr Tudor Williams and Mrs Lloyd Jones. Technically there is no need to cross-refer from Tudor Williams and Lloyd Jones, but sometimes this is desirable. Moreover, some such names are so commonly thought of as double-barrelled, with the emphasis even on the first part, that it would be perverse to apply the rule to them rigidly. Common sense demands that Lloyd George and Bonar Law be indexed under Lloyd and Bonar, although with cross-references from George and Law. In many cases it is impossible, without more research than the importance of the matter would justify, to determine whether or not the first part of an unhyphenated English compound name is a genuine surname. One is more likely to be right if one assumes that it is not and indexes under the second part, but there should be a cross-reference from the first.

Compound surnames are very rarely encountered in medieval records, and some of those that seem to be probably result from an error. *Ricardus Strynger Whyte* is usually the result of miscopying *Ricardus Strynger et Ricardus Whyte*, while *Johannes Smyht Bexle* is almost certainly an error for *Johannes Smyht de Bexle*. When the indexer knows from other evidence that the scribe was in error, he can index the person or persons according to what should have been written, whether or not this is explained, as it should be, in a footnote in the text; for example

Smith (Smyht), John, [of] Bexhill, 116
Bexhill (Bexle), Sussex, Smith of, q.v.

But if there is no such evidence it is as well to index exhaustively, as in

Stringer White (Strynger Whyte),
Richard, 232
White (Whyte), Richard Stringer
(Strynger), 232

(i) *Alphabetical Order of Surnames*

By contrast with place names, surnames are not repeated for each separate individual or even family, everyone with the same surname coming in the same entry. The problem of homonyms is therefore less acute, although not entirely absent as will be seen in the next section, and homonymous surnames of different nationalities must each have its own entry with the name repeated. Nevertheless the alphabetising of surnames can present problems. Those arising from modern names with prefixes have already been considered: when the prefix comes first in the index entry, prefix and main element should be regarded as a single word for determining alphabetical order (IV g). So should hyphenated names and names containing an apostrophe, both hyphens and apostrophes being ignored. Thus the order of the following names is correct

> O'Connor, Patrick, 563
> Odiham, Hants, 13, 272
> Ogg, Joseph, 316
> O'Malley, Richard, 662
> Ongar, High, Essex, 227
> Orde, William, 116
> Orde-Brown, William, 353
> Ordell, Matthew, 16
> O'Reilly, Thomas, 136
> Orton, Joseph, 55
> O'Sullivan, Agnes, 319

Likewise accented letters do not affect alphabetical order, although if two names are otherwise identical it is convenient to put the one with an accent second, for example Müller after Muller. Sometimes words containing the umlaut will be found alphabetised as though the letter 'e' followed the vowel with the umlaut, but the practice is confusing in indexes to British records.

Whether the alphabetical arrangement of the index is word by word or letter by letter (see VII b), the treatment of names beginning 'M'', 'Mc' and 'Mac', which are usually Scottish or Irish ones, is identical. They should all be arranged as though they began 'Mac',[6] the result being a sequence such as this

> McPartland, Alan, 772
> Macphail, John, 18
> McPhee, Alice, 54, 333
> Macpherson, Thomas, 8
> M'Quade, William, 666

Similarly all surnames, and also place names, beginning with 'St' should be alphabetised as though it were spelled out as 'Saint'. Thus the surname St John and the place name St Andrews would come in alphabetical order among any other Saints shortly after Saighton, and never after Stixwould and Standon. Equivalent foreign names, of persons and places, should be treated in the same way and alphabetised as though spelled out as San, Santa, Sao, and so on. Saint and its foreign equivalents are separate words for the word-by-word system of alphabetising, so that the surname St Paul and the parish of St Winnow come before Saintonge. Finally, places and, particularly, persons beginning with 'St' must be carefully distinguished from the Christian saints. The surname St John and St John's, Newfoundland, are indexed under 'S', whereas St John the Baptist is indexed under John, as is explained in the next section.

[6] Pre-1750 Scottish names should, however, all begin with the standardised form 'Mc' (see IV o).

(j) *Forenames as Index Entries*

There are certain categories of people who are always or sometimes indexed under their forenames. Of these, early Welshmen and Jews, and orientals are reserved for later consideration (IV p, q). The others, which are dealt with here, are saints, popes, sovereigns and members of their families, friars, and people who are only or usually known by their forenames, such as Raphael, or, in the early Middle Ages and before the Conquest, who had no surnames. When they have surnames under which they were, or sometimes still are, well known, as in the case of first generation monarchs or recently canonised saints, there should be cross-references from them, for example

> Bonaparte *see* Napoleon
> More, Sir Thomas *see* Thomas More,
> St

When there are persons in various of these categories with the same forename, the forename must be repeated for each separate person and it is recommended that they be arranged in the following order: biblical saints, other saints, popes, emperors, kings of England (who are just called 'king' unless it is necessary to differentiate them from kings of other countries with the same name), kings of other countries in alphabetical order of their countries, other members of sovereign houses again in alphabetical order of their countries, friars, and others known by their forenames; and the same name used as a surname comes at the end. When there are two or more popes of the same name they should follow each other in numerical order, and the same rule applies to monarchs of the same country. Thus a series might run

> John, St, the Baptist, 121, 124
> John, St, of the Cross, 123
> John X, pope, 59
> John XII, pope, 676
> John, king of England, 19, 64
>   brothers of *see* Geoffrey; Richard I
> John II, king of Scotland, 59, 177
> John, Augustus, 82
>   Eric, 317

As mentioned above (IV a), there is no point in indexing persons occurring in the text only as forenames because of the illegibility of the manuscript or an omission by the clerk.

It will be appreciated that in all the examples in this chapter forenames have been given in their modern English forms. It is recommended that this be done for all English persons, whether the forenames are indexed by themselves, as in this section, or with surnames. We have already seen (IV c) that *Johannes* in a transcript is translated as John for the index, and similarly Symon in a calendar or list should be indexed as Simon. When there are doubts, for example as to whether *Jacobus* should in a particular case be rendered as James or Jacob, it is best to give the manuscript form in brackets after the one chosen, and this is also advisable when the manuscript form is unusual.

Foreign forenames in editions of British records should either be anglicised or left in their modern foreign forms, depending upon how the people concerned are generally known in England. Thus popes are John and not Giovanni, French kings are John and Henry rather than Jean and Henri, and Raphael should be preferred to Raffaello, although cross-references can be included where it is thought desirable and must always be given if the foreign form appears in the text, in which case it should also be added in brackets after the English version in the main entry. But it would be pedantic to render the French kings Louis as Lewis, particularly Louis Philippe as Lewis Philip. It is also useful to keep the forenames of lesser known foreigners in their foreign spellings, if only to show their nationality at a glance.

(k) *Forenames as Subentries*

Under each surname entry the forenames of the different individuals must be set out as subentries in alphabetical order. As already stated (IV a), persons whose forenames are unknown come first of all. Every forename, when known, must be spelled out and not left as an initial, however it may appear in the text, although any letters of such names derived from other sources should be in square brackets. Second and subsequent forenames are often useful for alphabetising, John Alexander, for example, following plain John and preceding John Francis. But when there are persons whose forenames are known only by initials, they precede those with known forenames beginning with the same letters. A typical run of names is

> Fuller, J, 77-81
> J W, 331
> John, 590-1
> John Alexander, 12
> John F, 718
> John Francis, 662
> John Francis Makepeace, 54, 79

Titles such as Lord, Dr, Mrs, Rev and Sir, and military ranks (Sgt, Lieut, Captain, Major, etc.), all of which precede the forenames, are of very minor importance in determining the order of persons sharing a surname. Alphabetical order depends primarily on the forenames, and the last example might have correctly run

> Fuller, Major J, 77-81
> Mrs J W, 331
> John, 590-1
> Dr John Alexander, 12
> Rev John F, 718
> Sir John Francis, 662
> Lord John Francis Makepeace, 54,
> 79

Some indexes have such titles in italics, but that attracts unnecessary attention to them and there is hardly ever any real possibility of confusing titles with forenames, even in the case of Americans named Earl and Duke. Others have them after the forenames: instead of

> Robertson, Captain James, 154

they have

> Robertson, James, captain, 154

but that is an unnecessary inversion. A few inexplicably combine the use of italics with inversion.

Occasionally, however, titles and ranks can usefully distinguish persons of identical surname and forenames, who should be arranged in alphabetical order of the titles and not, as is sometimes advised, in hierarchical order which is bound to have a subjective element in it. Hierarchical order would be

> Johnson, Lord John, 77
> > Sir John, 619
> > Rev John, 350
> > Dr John, 11, 821
> > John, 6, 11, 821

The recommended alphabetical order is

> Johnson, John, 6, 11, 821
> > Dr John, 11, 821
> > Lord John, 77
> > Rev John, 350
> > Sir John, 619

those without titles preceding those with them.

Persons with identical names are more frequently distinguished from each other in other ways: in terms of their near relatives, their occupations or, most often, the places where they lived, all of which information can usefully be given under their names anyway if it is in the text; and by their dates or numbers in the case of peers. These are complex matters which will be considered fully in later sections (IV l-n).

When space is very short the most frequently occurring forenames can be abbreviated throughout the index, except for those few persons who are indexed by them (see IV j, p). Particularly in the Middle Ages Christian names, especially those of men, were fairly few and much space can be saved by shortening the commonest. The following abbreviations are suggested as appropriate, whenever the names occur sufficiently frequently to warrant their use

Alex	Alexander	Greg	Gregory	Phil	Philip
Ant	Anthony *or*	Hen	Henry	Ray	Raymond
	Antony	Hum	Humphrey	Reg	Reginald
Bart	Bartholomew	Jas	James	Reyn	Reynold
Chas	Charles	Jn	John	Ric	Richard
Chris	Christopher	Kath	Katherine	Rob	Robert
Clem	Clement	Ken	Kenneth	Rog	Roger
Dan	Daniel	Lawr	Lawrence	Rol	Roland
Edm	Edmund	Len	Leonard	Ron	Ronald
Edw	Edward	Margt	Margaret	Sam	Samuel
Eliz	Elizabeth	Margy	Margery	Sid	Sidney
Flo	Florence	Mat	Matthew	Stan	Stanley
Fred	Frederick	Mic	Michael	Thos	Thomas
Geo	George	Nat	Nathaniel	Tim	Timothy
Geof	Geoffrey	Nic	Nicholas	Wal	Walter
Gert	Gertrude	Ol	Oliver	Wm	William

In certain indexes other names may be worth abbreviating, although with the exception of John names of four letters or less should be written in full. Also 'sen' may be used for 'the elder' and 'jun' for 'the younger'. If space is extremely short 'd', 's' and 'w' can be used for 'daughter', 'son' and 'wife', but this is not generally recommended: indexes should not look as though they are written in shorthand or code. On the principle that punctuation in an index should be kept to the minimum (see X a), no full stops are required after these abbreviations: they are all clearly abbreviations, and most will be followed immediately by a comma. Those recommended should be readily understandable, but a table of abbreviations used, such as that set out above, should always be printed at the beginning of the index. In that they are employed solely to save space, abbreviations will normally be used only with the most economical kind of lay out—the paragraph arrangement of entries, which will be described later (XI d).

(l) *Relationships*

There is a strong case for including all simple relationships in the index, although never long genealogical trees occupying line after line. If space is very short it is just permissible to omit the simple relationships, unless they are essential to distinguish persons of identical name, and to index John son of Richard Smith merely as

> Smith, John, 27

But it might then be felt essential to have another entry under Smith, reading

> Richard, 27

If there were no other references in the text to Richard no space would be saved in this case, although over the whole index there would inevitably be some economy, especially with the use of paragraphed entries (see XI d). More seriously, the second subentry gives the misleading impression that Richard Smith occurs in the text in his own right, whereas he is only mentioned to describe his son. It is therefore preferable in such cases to have the relationship stated in the index. Some indexers would have the entry in the form

> Smith, John son of Richard, 27

while others prefer

> Smith, Richard, John son of, 27

The first is less clumsy and more straightforward. Moreover, John, who is the relevant person, is named before Richard and he will therefore be in his correct alphabetical position among the Smiths, where he will first be sought, and also adjacent to any other John Smiths from whom he must anyway be distinguished. On the other hand, a single individual often has many relatives described by their relationship to him. To have them dispersed among the other Smiths obscures the fact that they are inter-related, and how, especially if they occur in different places in the text; whereas to bring them all together under Richard not only makes the relationship clear but also shows that some of the references are the same, as they will inevitably be, thereby obviating unnecessary searches in passages already consulted. A few examples may make this clearer. An entry compiled under the first system might run

> Smith, Alexander son of Richard, 27
> > Alice wife of John, 90
> > Alice wife of Richard, 27
> > Bartholomew, tanner, 992
> > Clement, of Coventry, 62
> > David, bailiff of Bristol, 633
> > David, [of Nottingham], 29
> > John, of Droitwich, 90
> > John son of Richard, [of Nottingham],
> > > 32, 65
> > Matthew, 3
> > Richard, 27, 65, 109
> > Richard son of Richard, 109
> > Robert son of John, 90
> > William son of John, 90

The omission of a comma after the first forename when one person is described as related to another, which is desirable on the principle that unnecessary punctuation must be omitted as well as looking better and making for ease of reading, necessitates the repetition of the same forename in the following sub-entry: a practice which is always desirable, and which is essential in paragraphed entries. Not to repeat it when there is no comma, but merely to indent further, would imply that the whole of the previous complex of forenames was to be understood by the indentation. For example

          Smith, John, 29
             Richard son of Richard, 109
             son of William, 392

strictly means that the last reference is to a Richard son of Richard son of William Smith.

Under the second system our main entry would run

          Smith, Bartholomew, tanner, 992
             Clement, of Coventry, 62
             David, bailiff of Bristol, 633
             David, [of Nottingham], 29
             John, of Droitwich, 90
                Alice wife of, 90
                Robert son of, 90
                William son of, 90
             Matthew, 3
             Richard, 27, 65, 109
                Alexander son of, 27
                Alice wife of, 27
                John son of, [of Nottingham], 32, 65
                Richard son of, 109

In fact this entry could be made more concise, if slightly less clear, by organising the entries dependent upon John and Richard as follows

          Smith, John, of Droitwich, and Alice his
             wife and Robert and William his
             sons, 90
             Richard, 27, 65, 109
                Alexander son and Alice wife of, 27
                John son of, [of Nottingham], 32, 65
                Richard son of, 109

Incidentally, if the last reference had been 27 instead of 109 Richard should still have come after John for reasons of alphabetical order and not have been united with Alexander and Alice in the earlier sub-subentry.

Because both systems have merits and demerits, the best course is to combine their merits and eliminate most of the disadvantages by giving all the forenames in their correct alphabetical order with their references after them, but also cross-referring from the relatives in terms of whom they are described in the text. Our example would then read

          Smith, Alexander son of Richard, 27
             Alice wife of John, 90
             Alice wife of Richard, 27
             Bartholomew, tanner, 992

Smith (*contd*)
    Clement, of Coventry, 62
    David, bailiff of Bristol, 633
    David, [of Nottingham], 29
    John, of Droitwich, 90
        sons of *see* Robert; William
        wife of *see* Alice
    John son of Richard, [of Nottingham], 32, 65
    Matthew, 3
    Richard, 27, 65, 109
        sons of *see* Alexander; John; Richard
        wife of *see* Alice
    Richard son of Richard, 109
    Robert son of John, 90
    William son of John, 90

This takes up more space than either of the other systems, although there will rarely be many surnames covering as many individuals as our Smith and very often the only persons occurring with the same surname will all be members of the same family. Then the impossibility of confusing them with others and the absence of alphabetical interposition of other bearers of the name allow a much simpler treatment. But when the composite system of the last example is used, and it is here recommended, the extra space which it occupies can, if necessary, be saved, or more than saved, by adopting one or both of two practices: the paragraph arrangement (see XI d) and the abbreviation of commonly occurring forenames (IV k).

Wives and daughters provide a further indexing problem: whether, when all the information is supplied in the text, they should be indexed under their maiden or married names, or both, and also exactly how. When there is mention in the text of James Turner, his daughter Joan and her husband John Richards and there is no great shortage of space, the ideal index entries would be

    Richards, John, 66
        Joan wife of, and James Turner her
            father, 66
    Turner, James, 66
        Joan daughter of, and John Richards
            her husband, 66

But this is usually too extravagant, and the following are perfectly adequate

    Richards, John, and Joan his wife,
        daughter of James Turner, 66
    Turner, James, and Joan his daughter,
        wife of John Richards, 66

Indeed, there is no reason why the entries should not be in the even more concise form

    Richards, John, and Joan (Turner) his
        wife, 66
    Turner, James, and Joan (Richards)
        his daughter, 66

the words in brackets being obviously the other names by which Joan was or had been known. On the analogy of place-name and surname headings it is eminently proper that such 'obsolete' and 'variant' forms should be in round brackets. Less helpful is

Richards, John, and Joan (Turner) his
wife, 66
Turner, James, 66
daughter of *see* Richards

which saves no space and merely delays the searcher, although if a woman is to be indexed in one place only it should be under her husband rather than her father.

When a woman was married more than once and is described in the text in terms of two husbands, she can be indexed under both in one of the ways allowed above for a woman described as both daughter and wife, although if the third method is followed her second married name should not be anticipated in brackets under her first husband because it would be assumed to have been her maiden name. But if she should be described as the wife of three or more men, or as the wife of two and the daughter of a third, the enclosure of earlier and later names in brackets is impossible and index entries similar to the second Richards-Turner ones above are the most satisfactory. A series might run

Edwards, John, and Amelia his wife,
later wife successively of John
Bacon and Alan West, 79, 108
Bacon, John, and Amelia his wife, formerly wife of John Edwards and
later wife of Alan West, 79, 108
West, Alan, and Amelia his wife, formerly wife successively of John
Edwards and John Bacon, 79,
108

But when space is short Amelia's earlier and later marital career can be omitted from every entry.

Only very well known women should have cross-references from the names by which they are generally known when they appear in the text under others. For the rest, no research should be done to discover for the index married or maiden names which are not given in the text, and no relationships of men or women should be included in the index unless they occur in the text. It follows from this that although relationships sometimes distinguish persons with otherwise identical names, they are less generally useful for this purpose than offices, occupations and, particularly, places (see IV m, n).

(m) *Offices and Titles, Lay and Ecclesiastical*

Whereas popes and monarchs are indexed under their forenames, all other dignitaries and office holders, lay and ecclesiastical, are indexed primarily under their family names, whenever possible. It should nearly always be possible to discover the names of archbishops, bishops, peers and the great officers of state from the standard works of reference.[7] They should be identified and indexed

---

[7] Notably *Handbook of British Chronology*, 2nd edn (1961), ed Sir F. M. Powicke and E. B. Fryde (Royal Hist. Soc. Guides and Handbooks No. 2).

under their surnames even when these are not in the text. Thus when mention is made of the forfeiture of the earl of Arundel in the reign of Richard II, he must be identified and indexed as

Fitz Alan, Richard, earl of Arundel, 99

with the cross-reference

Arundel, earl of *see* Fitz Alan, Richard

Similarly if the text speaks of Thomas archbishop of York in the same reign, the index entries will be

Arundel, Thomas, archbishop of York, 167

York, archbishop of *see* Arundel, Thomas

and a commission to the chancellor in 1588 will produce

Hatton, Sir Christopher, chancellor, 296

Sometimes in a transcript the earl of Arundel will appear in forms such as the earl of Arondell. There is a case for then having two direct cross-references, namely

Arondell, earl of *see* Fitz Alan, Richard

Arundel (Arondell), earl of *see* Fitz Alan, Richard

thereby avoiding the cross-reference to a cross-reference

Arondell *see* Arundel

But there are stronger arguments against having the two direct cross-references. The first cross-reference gives the immediate impression that Arondell is the earl's correct title. Also, the cross-reference

Arondell *see* Arundel

will probably appear anyway for the town or rape or a surname and will then cover the earl. Moreover, most earldoms and other peerages are well known, and those interested in them will go straight to their modern spellings. This, of course, is not a problem for calendars and lists which have place names, including peerage titles, modernised, as advised above (III d).

When several of the Fitz Alan earls of Arundel occur in the text, it is best to use just the simple cross-reference

Arundel, earls of *see* Fitz Alan

The singular 'earl' would be positively misleading here, and for consistency it is therefore recommended that the plural be used in all such cases when more than one person is cross-referred to or will be found under any numerical references given. The singular will often be found in indexes in this context, presumably because there was never more than one earl at the time, which is not a sufficient reason.

The main Fitz Alan entry should contain all the earls mentioned. They should be in normal alphabetical order of forenames, earls with the same forenames being distinguished by the years during which they held the title in square brackets and being arranged in chronological order, thus

Fitz Alan, Edmund, earl of Arundel, 322

Richard, earl of Arundell, [1291-1302], 67, 212

Fitz Alan (*contd*)
Richard, earl of Arundel, [1330-
1376], 212
Richard, earl of Arundel, [1376-
1397], 212, 322
Thomas, earl of Arundel, 322

This is more immediately informative than to give the Richards numbers instead of dates. It is also unambiguous, whereas peers are numbered differently in different works of reference, *The Complete Peerage* starting a fresh numeration for each family and the *Handbook of British Chronology* using a continuous numeration which takes no account of different families even when the title and rank of the peerage change. There is no need to provide dates when there is no possibility of confusion, as when there was ever only one earl with a particular forename or when the only earl in the index with a particular forename flourished in the period covered by the volume. There is never any need to provide the dates of bishops' tenures of their sees, as is sometimes done, since they are adequately distinguished by their different surnames. Nothing superfluous should be added to indexes to record publications, which are quite large enough anyway: they are aids to the use of the text, not potted biographies. But it is not superfluous to give both surname and title of a peer when they are the same. Indeed,

Stafford, Henry earl of, 17

is inadequate, because potentially ambiguous. It should read

Stafford, Henry, earl of Stafford, 17

although a cross-reference from 'Stafford, earl of', which would be adjacent, would only be necessary if there were also other earls of Stafford in the text with different surnames, in which case the Stafford surname should be included in the cross-reference.

The only exceptions to the rule that archbishops, bishops, peers and the great officers of state should be indexed under their surnames are when it is uncertain which of several past holders of such a title or office is meant, and, more often, when the text refers not specifically to the holder at the date of the document or of a defined earlier time, but to the holder whoever he may be, earlier, now and later. For example, references to land held of the bishop of Chichester imply a continuing tenurial relationship: that if the current bishop died the next day, his successor would succeed to the lordship of the land; and similarly with suit of court owed to the earl of Oxford. The index entries would merely be

Chichester, bishop of, 622
Oxford, earl of, 334

and comparable references to continuing duties of the chancellor require corresponding entries in the Subject Index (see V e). Very often a volume contains references of each kind, in which case the index should have entries like these

Arundel, earl of, 33, 69, 122
See also Fitz Alan, Richard
Fitz Alan, Richard, earl of Arundel, 17,
28-31, 644

or perhaps

Arundel, earls of, 33, 69, 122
See also Fitz Alan

with various Fitz Alan earls under that head.

Ecclesiastical dignitaries and lay and ecclesiastical officials other than the eminent ones so far considered need never be identified if they are not named in the text. In very many cases it would be difficult or impossible to do so. If completely anonymous, they can only figure in the index under their place, master or office, for example

> Oxford, Oxon, bailiff of, 522
> Bray, Berks, vicar of, 11
> Signet Office, clerk of, 413

and likewise if only their forenames are given

> Bexhill (Bexle), Sussex, manor, Henry
>   bailiff of, 332
> Fitz Alan, Richard, earl of Arundel,
>   John steward of, 694

When such officials are named in the text, the main entries must be under their surnames thus

> Marsh (Mersshe), Henry atte, bailiff of
>   the manor of Bexhill, 332
> Smith (Smyth), John, steward of
>   Richard Fitz Alan, earl of Arun-
>   del, 694
> Well (Welle), Richard atte, vicar of
>   Bray, 29

For economy the middle one could be cut to

> Smith (Smyth), John, steward of the
>   earl of Arundel, 694

On the analogy with the higher officials and dignitaries there should also be the following cross-references

> Bexhill (Bexle), Sussex, manor, bailiff
>   of *see* Marsh, Henry atte
> Fitz Alan, Richard, earl of Arundel,
>   steward of *see* Smith, John
> Bray, Berks, vicar of *see* Well, Richard
>   atte

Once again, for economy the cross-references can be to surnames alone, although this is slightly less helpful and should only be done (and then consistently throughout the index) if space is very limited.

But the analogy with the higher officials and dignitaries is not exact. The references to every higher official are frequently numerous so that the cross-references to them are justifiable, especially as their eminence means that searchers will often be interested in only one of them. By contrast, anyone who looks up the bailiff of a manor or the vicar of a parish under the places will almost certainly be interested in any bailiff or vicar. A single cross-reference in such circumstances is tiresome, three or four much more so. There is therefore a strong case for dispensing with cross-references to lesser officials and having numerical references instead, so that our last entries would read

> Bexhill (Bexle), Sussex, manor, bailiff
>   (*named*) of, 332
> Fitz Alan, Richard, earl of Arundel,
>   steward (*named*) of, 694
> Bray, Berks, vicar (*named*) of, 29

The inclusion of the word 'named' is useful for those who would not wish to pursue a reference to an anonymous office holder.

A slightly more complex entry often encountered is of this kind

> Sussex, county, coroners of, 1, 6, 79.
> *See also* Green, Richard; Pres-
> ton, Thomas; White, Thomas

This, of course, is only permissible if the references under the specific coroners' names are different from those given under Sussex. It is intolerable to ask the searcher to turn to three names, only for him to find that he has no new references. Entries 1, 6, and 79 should mention unnamed Sussex coroners, although one of the named coroners may also appear in one or more of them; and two of the coroners may appear under the same reference. One occasionally encounters the above entry in the following form

> Sussex, county, coroners of, 1, 6, 79,
> (Thomas Preston) 88, (Thomas
> White) 96, 222, (Richard Green)
> 154

or, more expansively,

> Sussex, county, coroners of, 1, 6, 79
> (Thomas Preston) 88
> (Thomas White) 96, 222
> (Richard Green) 154

The forenames can be omitted from either, but both forms are complicated and they can get impossibly involved when there are many named coroners, some of whom share some references but not others. On balance, the first type of entry is better than the other two, but best of all is the simple entry

> Sussex, county, coroners of, 1, 6, 79;
> (*named*) 88, 96, 154, 222

It saves space, is cheaper and provides the searcher with direct references. As argued above in respect of the bailiff of the manor of Bexhill, it is reasonable to assume that anyone turning to the entry 'Sussex, county, coroners of' is interested in the office of coroner in that county irrespective of the particular holders, whereas anyone interested in a particular coroner will go straight to his name. Incidentally, the entry 'Sussex, county, coroner of' can never be justified unless just one coroner appears in the text since there were always at least two in office at any time—another reason for using the plural whenever more than one official or dignitary is meant.

One justification for indexing all title and office holders primarily under their family names is that it is useful for different members of the same family to appear as close together as possible in the index. More important, surnames and forenames are normally constant, whereas many people had several titles and a large number of offices, either concurrently or consecutively. This is particularly true of archbishops, bishops, peers and the great officers of state. It is obviously essential that all the references to a person should be brought together in a single entry, and the surname is the natural heading for them, or the forename in the case of popes and monarchs. But it is also desirable that the references to an individual should be related specifically to his relevant titles and capacities and not all lumped together. Such individuals should therefore have subentries or sub-subentries like these

> Henry V, king, 214-412 *passim*
>   as prince of Wales, 36, 40, 201
> Arundel, Thomas, archbishop of Can-
>   terbury, 677, 702
>   archbishop of York, 592
>   bishop of Ely, 33
> Wolsey, Thomas, cardinal, archbishop
>   of York, 99, 102, 104, 166
>   chancellor, 116, 392, 400
>   legate *a latere*, 155

In the first two cases the different positions were held consecutively, but Wolsey held his concurrently. Each official position in either case must have a separate subentry, unless the references are identical when two or even more can and should be combined, as are cardinal and archbishop under Wolsey, where, indeed, cardinal can be understood to be included with the other subentries as well. There are three possible ways of arranging such subentries: in chronological order; where relevant, in hierarchical order, which is usually but not necessarily the same and can supplement a chronological arrangement when offices were held in plurality; and in alphabetical order. We have already rejected hierarchical in favour of alphabetical order for homonymous persons (IV k), and do so here for the same reasons. Chronological order is recommended for such entries in General Indexes (see VI a), but for an Index of Persons and Places, which is normally to be preferred (VI b) and which is primarily arranged alphabetically, alphabetical order should only be rejected even for sub-subentries if there are over-riding reasons, which certainly do not exist in this case. The above entries therefore have their subentries in alphabetical order. This is even true of the first, since the second line must be read as 'the king as prince of Wales'; and of the last, where cardinal and archbishop share the same references and come in that order because cardinal relates to the other subentries as well.

Wolsey held a succession of bishoprics before becoming archbishop of York, but if they are not mentioned in the text they do not warrant a place in the index. As already stated (IV l), indexes are no places for potted biographies: just as no research should be done to discover a person's relationships, so should his official or social career be ignored.

Foreign nobles and officials can be indexed exactly as their British equivalents, but there is the complication of having to decide whether or not to anglicise their titles. The rule is that both secular and ecclesiastical offices and titles should be anglicised whenever there is an exact English equivalent. It would be as absurd to have

> Lisieux, évêque de, 927

in an index to British records, as to have

> France, roi de *see* Louis XIV

But only those titles which are traditionally known in an English form should be given in English. It is more useful and safer to leave lesser known ones, such as the comte de Montlaur, in their foreign forms. This, of course, except in the case of full transcripts, is less an indexing problem than one for the editor of the text.

Finally, the indexer must always remember that some searchers will be interested only in a person's family and others only in his official career. It is for this reason that every individual's offices and titles which are mentioned in the text

are given as subentries after the name in the index. For the same reason in a
volume of inquisitions it is useful to note in the index which people occur only
or sometimes as jurors, and in a volume of charters which ones occur as witnesses.
As there will be many in both categories, the use of the letters 'j' and 'w' after the
relevant names, or before the relevant references when they relate to some and
not to others, is an adequate warning, always provided that their significance is
explained at the beginning of the index. Other routine references can also be
distinguished. Thus rather than a composite entry reading

> Cecil, Sir Robert, letters from, 8, 16, 17,
>   19, 20, 30

it is better to distinguish the routine from the more personal in such a way as

> Cecil, Sir Robert, letters from, 16, 17,
>   20
>   letters signed by, as Privy Council-
>   lor, 8, 19, 30

when the distinction is clear from the text.

A further aid to users is not to merge a man's subentries into a single alphabetical sequence, when some describe his official career and others concern his
relatives, normally daughters, parents, sons and wife or wives. Such a single
sequence might run

> Paris, John, 24, 992
>   alderman of London, 21
>   Anne wife of, 24, 632
>   daughters of, 632
>   mayor of London, 256-7
>   Robert son of, 632
>   sheriff of London, 167
>   William son of, 632

This is one of the few cases in which strict alphabetical order is less defensible
than another arrangement: here, two alphabetical sequences, the offices in one
and the relatives in the other. Many searchers will be interested either in Paris
in his official capacities or in his family, and they will be best served by the
separation of the two distinct elements. Those few who are interested in both
will need to follow up all the references however they are arranged, and even
they will probably find the arrangement in two groups helpful because logical.

The decision as to which group should come first is not easy to make. If there
are references to the main character as a private individual they will follow
naturally on from his name, as in the last example, so that there is a case for
putting his relations next and his offices last. On the other hand there is probably
a slightly stronger case for having the offices immediately following the personal
references, so that all the references to the principal person in his various
capacities come together and those to other people come at the end. It is therefore
recommended that the last example should read

> Paris, John, 24, 992
>   alderman of London, 21
>   mayor of London, 256-7
>   sheriff of London, 167
>   Anne wife of, 24, 632
>   daughters of and Robert and Wil-
>   liam sons of, 632

(n) *Homonymous Persons*

We have already seen (IV k) that persons with the same surnames and forenames can be distinguished from each other by their styles: Lord, Sir, Dr, Mr, Major, and so on. But more frequently they are distinguished in other ways. One such way is by relationships stated in the text, as in

Roper, Alan son of John, 16
Alan son of William, 22

Another is by their offices, for example

Roper, Alan, bailiff of Oxford, 67
Alan, mayor of York, 133

The repetition of the name Alan is essential, because

Roper, Alan, bailiff of Oxford, 67
mayor of York, 133

indicates that the same Alan Roper succeeded in achieving these two offices, unlikely as it is. Yet another method of differentiating is by occupations, which, like offices, should be given after personal names anyway, if space permits, whenever they are in the text, whether or not they are necessary in the index to distinguish people. An example is

Roper, Alan, goldsmith, 522
Alan, tanner, 953

Most commonly, however, people with identical names are distinguished by the places where they lived. Such places are sometimes explicitly stated in the text, as in the phrase 'Alan Roper of Coventry', while on other occasions it is quite clear from the context that an Alan Roper lived in Nottingham although this is not stated in so many words. They should be indexed as follows

Roper, Alan, of Coventry, 336
Alan, [of Nottingham], 76

Places, like Nottingham, which are supplied by the indexer should only be included in the index when it is necessary to differentiate between people, and there is no need for a cross-reference from Nottingham to Roper. Indeed, it is axiomatic that there will be a direct reference under Nottingham to the same entry in the text, otherwise Nottingham could not have been supplied. But, if space allows, descriptions such as 'of Coventry' should always be included, and there should either be a cross-reference in the form

Coventry, Warw, Roper of, *q.v.*

or, if Roper is one of a number of Coventry men so described,

Coventry, Warw, people (*named*) of,
336

This type of entry is different from that for an official of a place, for whom a direct reference under the place was said above (IV m) to be always preferable to a cross-reference to the person. Here the cross-reference is better, because the searcher is thereby warned that he must not expect a mention in the text of Coventry for its own sake, but only as a description of a man named Roper. Of course the same is true if there are, say, four or more persons of Coventry so described, but to replace a composite cross-reference by a single numerical reference saves space and also prevents a searcher from having to turn to four or more names only to find the same reference each time. Not only that, but whereas the description of one man as being 'of Coventry' is generally of little importance to the student of Coventry, the simultaneous occurrence of four or more such men is significant and would justify a direct reference under Coventry.

It is therefore recommended that when up to three people are described in the text in terms of a place they should be cross-referred to in the last subentry of that place, but that four or more require the subentry 'people (*named*) of' and a direct reference.

When it is essential to economise ruthlessly on space and there is no other person with an identical name, it is permissible to index Alan Roper of Coventry merely as

Roper, Alan, 336

and to include a similar numerical reference under Coventry

Coventry, Warw, 336

but this is much less useful. In a volume containing records relating to a whole country it is more useful to include the place under the person as a general rule than in a volume devoted to the records of a single county or borough; although in the latter category there will always be a number of very common local surnames whose holders will have to be distinguished in one way or another, most often by their places of residence.

When a person is described in the text as being of a place which cannot be identified, or cannot be firmly identified, that fact must be indicated typographically under the person in the same way as under the place itself, except that the word '*unidentified*' is unnecessary. Thus, persons from three of the places used as examples in section III g should be indexed as

Roper, Alan, of 'Bercrcra', 24

Alan, of Houghton ?Conquest, 76

Alan, of Sutton, 76

It is often impossible to tell from the text exactly where people whom it is essential to distinguish lived. When there is nothing else by which to differentiate them, the county or borough (but not a smaller place) with which they are associated in the text can be added to their entries as follows

Roper, Alan, [Norfolk], 26

Alan, [Suffolk], 67

The absence of the word 'of' means that the indexer is not committing himself to the statement that these were men who lived in Norfolk and Suffolk respectively. Indeed, he is not even saying that they were necessarily two different men. He is merely avoiding the danger of bringing together under one name references which may relate to two men. He is actually saying that an Alan Roper was active in Norfolk or in connection with Norfolk, and that either the same man or another was similarly associated with Suffolk. Such entries should come after all those for persons with identical names who are more firmly described geographically, thus

Roper, Alan, of Coventry, 336

Alan, [of Nottingham], 76

Alan, of Oswestry, 567

Alan, [Norfolk], 26

Alan, [Suffolk], 67

There is no question of cross-referring from Norfolk and Suffolk to Roper: it would be even less justifiable than a cross-reference from Nottingham. Because the counties are describing persons and not places and are therefore in a more unusual setting, they should not be abbreviated quite so ruthlessly as was recommended for places (III h). The important thing is that the county should be immediately recognizable as such. Northants and Bucks are adequate, but Norf, Midd and Warw should be extended.

Whenever possible, people with identical names should be distinguished by strictly comparable qualifications, a place or county being normally the most convenient. Thus the entry

> Roper, Alan, 534
> Alan, bailiff of Oxford, 67
> Alan, of Coventry, 336
> Alan son of William, 22
> Alan, tanner, 953

is far from ideal in that only the second and third references necessarily relate to different men, although the chances are that all five are different and in the absence of better information even the descriptions given may well be more useful for knowledgeable searchers than they are to the uninitiated. But the insertion, if possible, of a place or county in square brackets after those not defined in terms of a place would produce the much more valuable entry

> Roper, Alan, bailiff of Oxford, 67
> Alan, of Coventry, 336
> Alan, [Worcs], 534
> Alan son of William, [of Chelms-
> ford], 22
> Alan, tanner, [Yorks], 953

The order of the individuals here given is one of a number of possible sequences, none of which is indisputably the best. There is a case for having 'Alan, [Worcs]' at the end, but he is placed third in order to be adjacent to the only other Alan who is described merely in terms of a place. There is similarly a case for having 'Alan son of William' at the end, but equally the absence of a comma after Alan can be ignored for the purposes of alphabetising in such instances.

In every index there will be persons bearing the same name, about whom the text provides no information, either directly or implicitly, whereby they can be differentiated in the index. When, in such cases, there is no doubt that they are two people, as, for example, when one continued to act after the other is recorded as having died, the best method of indexing them is as follows

> Roper, Alan, 532
> Alan, (*another*), 676

or, where relevant,

> Roper, Alan, of Coventry, 336
> Alan, [of Nottingham], 76
> Alan, [of Nottingham], (*another*),
> 676

When it is most likely, but there is no conclusive proof, that they are two persons, they can be indexed as

> Roper, Alan, 532
> Alan, (?*another*), 676

and when it is most likely, but not certain, that they are one and the same, as

> Roper, Alan, 532
> Alan, (?*same*), 676

Occasionally it may be clear that there are several people of the same name who are incapable of individual description. They can be simply rendered

> Roper, Alan, (*various persons*), 76, 99,
> 336, 532, 676, 701, 1004

or, if some can be distinguished and others cannot,

Roper, Alan, of Coventry, 336

Alan, [of Nottingham], 76

Alan, (*other persons*), 99, 532, 701, 1004

Alternatively, the last subentry might read

Alan, (*another person*), 99, 532, 701, 1004

or, when one or more of the references could conceivably refer to one of the Alan Ropers specifically described,

Alan, (*?another person*), 99, 532, 701, 1004

or

Alan, (*?other persons*), 99, 532, 701, 1004

(o) *Scottish Names*

These have already been mentioned in the context of the alphabetising of names beginning with 'Mc', 'Mac' and 'M'' (IV i). Two further matters remain to be considered. One concerns those Scottish surnames which have territorial designations. They should each have a separate index entry and should be arranged in alphabetical order of the territories after any persons with the surnames alone. A typical series is

Stewart, James, bailiff of Edinburgh, 62

Stewart of Appin, Alexander, 22

Stewart of Ardureck, John, 199

Stewart of Fasnacloich, Andrew, 237

Apart from the fact that such names may be regarded as virtually composite surnames, this format and order are far more satisfactory than if the territorial designations followed the forenames in that they keep the members of each family together. No cross-references from the territories are required.

The other matter concerns Gaelic patronymics, which are encountered mainly in Scottish records. The practice of the Scottish Record Office is to cross-refer copiously: for example, to have cross-references between the same 'Mc' and 'Nin' or 'Nc' patronymics, as follows

McDonochie VcEan, Robert, 42

See also NinDonochie

NinDonochie VcEan, Elspeth, 217

See also McDonochie

They also recommend a reference for each 'Mc' and 'Vc' form and the ordinary surname of the same person, as in

McDouill Eir VcDoniche, Ewan, 76

VcDoniche, Ewan McDouill Eir, 76

and again

McWilliam McAllan, Edward Grant, 122

McAllan, Edward Grant McWilliam, 122

Grant McWilliam McAllan, Edward, 122

They prefer names beginning 'Mc', 'Nin' and 'Nc' to be so indexed, however they are spelt in the text. This is a good way of standardising pre-1750 surnames, but later ones should be left in the preferred spelling of each individual family.

(p) *Welsh Names*
It has been recommended (IV c) that forenames should normally not be used as index entries for early records, contrary to French and some English practice, even for cross-referring to second names; and this whether or not the second names were common to the whole family and were inherited and passed on. This is because Christian names were so few, and Englishmen of the past are not thought of primarily by their Christian names. The Welsh, however, prefer to have medieval Welshmen indexed under their first names, and it is reasonable to adopt this practice because Welsh surnames were very late in evolving and throughout the Middle Ages Welshmen were known only by primitive patronymics, although these often encompassed many generations. It would obviously be tedious to index Madoc ap Griffith ap Llewelyn ap Lloyd in any other way than straightforwardly under Madoc. This is out of pattern with what is recommended for early English patronymics (IV c), but the difference is that hardly any such Welsh names gave rise to a surname for the family.

Only at the end of the Middle Ages and in Tudor times can one see this development taking place with Welsh names. Then one still frequently finds Madoc ap Owen, but also Madoc Apowen, Madoc Bowen and, a little later, Madoc Owen—sometimes two or more of them together, linked by the word *alias*. The rule must therefore be that when in the text Welsh names are no longer all in the form of primitive patronymics, the patronymic parts can be indexed as if they were surnames. During the time when primitive patronymics and rudimentary surnames coexist, with fair numbers of each, mainly the Tudor period, it is probably best to cross-refer from the forename to the chosen surname in cases such as our Madoc, when there are primitive and more developed forms of the same name in the text. If all four forms given above appeared in the same volume in respect of the same man, the index entries would be

> Madoc ap Owen *see* Owen
> Apowen *see* Owen
> Bowen *see* Owen
> Owen (Apowen, Bowen), Madoc *alias*
>   Madoc ap, 63, 94, 225, 667

There is never any need to cross-refer from 'ap' when it is a separate word.

Because of the difficulties inherent in the indexing of Welsh names, it is recommended that a brief note be made at the beginning of the index stating how they are treated.

(q) *Jews, Arabs and Orientals*
Jewish and oriental names can present even greater difficulties than Welsh ones. Jews mentioned in early records are normally indexed under their forenames, even when any other name or description is known, which is not very often. With Arabs and orientals it is often impossible for the non-expert to know which is the forename and which the surname, and sometimes even which are titles. Useful guidance will be found in chapter four of *Training in Indexing*. When there remains any doubt, the last name can be regarded as the surname and the other or others as forenames, but it is a wise precaution to have a cross-reference

from the whole name given in the order in which it occurs in the text. Once again a prefatory note can be inserted explaining anything concerning the indexing of these names that is peculiar to the particular volume.

(r) *Other Foreign Names*

The purpose of this paragraph is merely to refer back to earlier sections of this chapter in which various aspects of the indexing of foreign, mainly Western European, names are considered. Foreign names with prefixes are dealt with in section (g), compound names very briefly in section (h), names beginning with the equivalent of Saint in section (i), foreign forenames at some length in section (j) and foreign nobles and officials in section (m).

Only three more points need be made. First, it is dangerous for the English indexer to attempt to apply any principles of standardisation to foreign surnames. Familiar historical figures should be indexed under the names by which they are best known, with cross-references from any other forms found in the text. But other foreigners should be indexed under one of the manuscript forms, with cross-references from any others. Secondly, the indexer must always be careful to avoid conflating English surnames and similar foreign ones into a single entry. Thus the French surname Sainte should never be conflated with the English surname Saint, but each must have its own entry. The danger is particularly great when there is an Englishman whose name is spelt Sainte and who must appear under Saint. Thirdly, when people are described in the text as being of a certain nationality and are not otherwise described, for example as being of a certain town, it is worth including the nationality in the index as follows

> Honeysett (Annessett), Adrian, French-
> man, 60[8]

---

[8] This somewhat unlikely entry is explained in *Sussex Notes and Queries*, xv (1958-62), 59-61; xvi (1963-7), 172-4.

CHAPTER V

SUBJECTS

(a) *What are Subjects?*

Whereas every person and place occurring in the text must be indexed, the Subject Index[1] will always be selective, although it should not be subjective. Whereas there is never any doubt as to which words represent persons and places, it is sometimes very difficult to decide what exactly are the subjects which need to be indexed: an Index of Subjects should be very much more than an index of objects, and some of the words under which subjects, particularly those of a more conceptual nature, should be indexed may not occur in the text at all. And whereas the indexing of persons and places is relatively straightforward in that there are clear rules which can be applied to them uniformly whatever the records may be, subjects do not lend themselves to such regimentation: they vary hierarchically from volume to volume according to the nature of the records, so that a subject which requires a long entry of its own in one volume may be represented by a minor subentry in another. These points will now be considered at greater length.

It is impossible for any Subject Index to be exhaustive, although the plethora of subjects and the complexity of their treatment in the indexes of some recent record publications suggest that an attempt has been made to include everything possible. This may represent an extreme reaction against the omission of all subjects from indexes to most early record publications or, alternatively, absolute determination that the choice of subjects should not be subjective. Certainly the indexer must avoid over-emphasising, and in some cases even including, matters which particularly interest him. Entries such as 'Surnames', subdivided into categories each containing long lists of names, 'Christian names, unusual', again with many names, and 'Language', perhaps divided into 'Latin words, unusual' and 'Vernacular words, unusual', are too much of a luxury for the normal index, especially if they are of great length as they tend to be. Surnames can always be found in the Index of Persons and Places, and the expert will want to arrange them in his own categories while the average user will not want them so ordered at all. Which Christian names are unusual will vary from county to county and from generation to generation. The text itself may not be representative of its time in this respect, and yet if the indexer tries to use any criteria as to which are unusual other than the infrequency of their occurrence in the text, he will inevitably introduce his own concept of the usual and the unusual into the index. Once again, the few experts will prefer to go through the Index of Persons and Places and make their own judgments.

With these and similar exceptions all subjects should be indexed. Equally important, they should be thoroughly indexed: any matter which is indexed at all should have a reference to every place in the text where it occurs. That is the general rule, but it is permissible and desirable to modify it by an intelligent use of the Introduction. The Subject Index and Introduction should be complementary. Common form and topics of frequent occurrence can easily swamp the important and the exceptional in a Subject Index. The most satisfactory practice

---

[1] This chapter is concerned only with separate Subject Indexes. The subject element in General Indexes is dealt with in the next, although many of the points are valid for both.

is to deal with some of them in the Introduction and then have a single reference to the Introduction under each in the Subject Index, instead of very many references to the text or '*passim*'. This practice is particularly useful for dealing with the nature, as distinct from the content, of the records transcribed or calendared, because an introductory passage can be much more full and informative than an index entry. Typical entries are

> Inquisitions, indented, ix-xi
> taken *ex officio*, xi-xiii
> Writs, witnessed by the guardian of
> England, xx

Such references to the Introduction do not merely save many lines of references to the text or the less useful '*passim*'; they also allow the less formal and routine matters concerning inquisitions and writs to stand out more clearly. This use of the Introduction means that the abnormal will feature in the index to a disproportionately great extent, which makes it essential that what is normal should be adequately explained in the Introduction. The normal and abnormal are not necessarily, of course, what the indexer would consider to be such in any circumstances, but merely what he finds to be normal and abnormal in his documents. It is a matter of fact, not of qualitative judgment.

Subject entries are normally of two kinds: those which arise naturally from the documents and relate to matters which they can be expected to illustrate; and others, perhaps concerning historical events of the period, which happen to be mentioned although there could have been no certainty, given the nature of the records, that they necessarily would be. In the first category come any relevant information about the records themselves, especially any unusual points of diplomatic; administrative matters, concerning the office or court which produced the documents, its relations with other institutions, and the officials of the parent office and any others mentioned; and those aspects of the history and the life of the period for which the records are certain to be a major source of information.

The distinction between these two main kinds of subject entries may be illustrated from the *Curia Regis Rolls*. The Subject Indexes to these volumes of thirteenth-century legal records must clearly have major subject groupings such as 'Actions', 'Courts', 'Crimes', 'Juries', 'Justices', 'Officers', 'Pleadings', 'Procedure', 'Records' and 'Writs', which are inevitable for documents of this type. It is also certain that the law suits will throw light on the economic and agrarian life of the times and that there must therefore be subject entries like 'Agriculture', 'Animals', 'Food and Drink', 'Household articles', 'Taxation' and 'Tenures and Services'. There are, however, many other topics which may or may not come up in the text, but which must be indexed if they do: 'Crusades' and 'Pilgrimages', for example, which the indexer may decide to bring under some more general heading such as 'Ecclesiastical matters'.

There is a particular value in indexing these last subjects, which, far from being the primary concern of the documents, are probably only mentioned incidentally and almost by chance. Such central topics as 'Actions', 'Procedure' and 'Writs' must, of course, loom large in indexes to *Curia Regis Rolls* volumes, and can be very useful entries when thoroughly edited by an expert in thirteenth-century law. But most users of these index entries will be other experts in that field, and they will often need to read the whole volume. Indeed, if the records were not published, they would almost certainly use the originals or photocopies of them. It is far different with the historian of the crusades or the searcher interested in pilgrimages. Not only would they never embark upon the original manuscripts, but they would be unlikely to read through the printed text of legal records on the off-chance of finding a stray mention of their subjects. But if crusades and pilgrimages appear in the Subject Index, such searchers can rapidly and painlessly obtain any relevant information from a class of records which would otherwise be closed to them. It is in this way that a sensibly comprehensive Subject Index can give a greater depth and range to a wide variety of historical writing; and the inclusion in it of the unusual entry is the supreme justification of the Subject Index and of record publishing.

The indexer should always bear this in mind. He can never be certain that a given class of records will never at any time be searched for particular subjects or aspects of history, however unlikely it is that historians will currently look for them there. He must therefore not exclude subjects which are unfashionable or not yet fashionable, as indexers fifty and more years ago frequently omitted matters concerning the social and economic life of the period of their documents, to the chagrin of many later historians.

As already mentioned, it is not always easy to recognize significant subjects, and one of the great dangers is that in some of the fields covered or touched on by his documents the indexer will index not subjects but words: that he will include all explicit mentions of a subject, although many may be of no great significance, while omitting important aspects of it because they occur in a form of words which does not immediately suggest that particular subject to the non-specialist. An example of this was discussed in the last chapter (IV a): the occurrence of the word 'king' or of his name in such a context as the taking of lands into the king's hand or into the hand of King Henry IV. This requires no entry under Henry IV in the Index of Persons and Places, but only a reference in the Index of Subjects under some such heading as 'Forfeitures' or 'Escheats'. The indexer must there-fore concentrate all the time less on the actual words used in the text than on their meaning, and, of course, the less concrete and more conceptual the subject the more difficult is this aspect of his job. He must bear in mind the subjects which users of the volume will be likely to look up, and recognize them whenever they occur in the text, however obliquely or allusively. Naturally, the more miscellaneous and wide-ranging the documents, the greater polymath must the indexer be and the more alert and aware must he remain, to ensure that he has collected all the references to every topic and has included none that is irrelevant. It follows from what has been said in this paragraph that a second danger confronting the subject indexer is that references to the same subject may be dispersed under several synonymous headings in the index—a matter which is discussed at greater length below (V c).

(b) *Grouping*
Whether and how to group subjects in an index are never easy decisions to make. There are two extremes. One is to have no groups at all, but to index every subject separately so that it will appear with references, not just a cross-reference, in its correct alphabetical position. The other is to reduce the Subject Index to a small number of large groups, perhaps no more than twenty. The first has the advantage that anyone interested in a small subject, like horses or epilepsy, will find his references without being redirected to another part of the index. But many searchers, probably more, will be interested in other animals or illnesses

as well, and their task is much increased by the absence of any grouping. Cross-references between each animal or disease and every other would often be lengthy and cumbersome, and therefore unjustifiable, although the indexer might feel obliged to cross-refer between horses, mares, colts and stallions. The alternative—to break away from the simple entry arrangement and to bring these few entries, and other comparable ones, together—is to introduce incipient grouping. Moreover, there will usually be some occurrences in the text of animals and illnesses in general, necessitating subject entries under those words or synonyms; and even if there are not, it is hard to justify having the particular animals and illnesses scattered throughout the index without cross-references from such general headings. Either way, the specific animals and illnesses might as well have all been grouped under those heads in the first place.

The second practice—of having a few large groups and no single entries—has several advantages. There need be no cross-references of any kind, but just a warning note at the beginning of the index: 'All subjects are grouped under the following headings: . . .' A second advantage is that much repetition of modifications can be avoided. For example, an entry might read

> Animals, 66, 72, 594
>> stolen, 59
>> types of
>>> cows, 13, 59, 76
>>> horses, 59, 82, 314
>>> oxen, 3, 59, 82
>>> sheep, 6, 16, 59

whereas under the first practice the following entries would be required

> Animals, 66, 72, 594. *See also* Cows;
>> Horses; Oxen; Sheep
>
> Cows, 13, 76
>> stolen, 59
> Horses, 82, 314
>> stolen, 59
> Oxen, 3, 82
>> stolen, 59
> Sheep, 6, 16
>> stolen, 59

Nevertheless, the second practice also has its drawbacks. One is that the groupings will often be so gigantic that there will be an almost inevitable tendency for them to be subdivided into subentries and sub-subentries at the very least. At worst they can become so complex as to be self-defeating, usable only by the indexer and perhaps not even by him after some lapse of time. As a rule, when it is felt necessary to number the subheadings the grouping is too large and should be split into its component parts, although it is true that numbers do facilitate cross-references to subentries if cross-references are used. Another disadvantage is that some subjects will almost certainly get forced into slightly unnatural relationships within groups which would not be everyone's choice for them, simply to ensure that everything is neatly in a group. Such subjects can be completely lost without cross-references, but their inclusion removes one of the main advantages of the system.

It therefore follows that the ideal Subject Index would contain the best of both systems and would lie somewhere between the two extremes, probably nearer to the second than to the first. It is recommended here that as many subjects as possible should be associated in groups, but that the classification should be natural and never forced. Kindred subjects gain enormously from juxtaposition: the value of the group entry is far greater than the total value of its component parts. But subentries in unnatural associations lose much, if not all, of their value. The classification of subjects should therefore never be arranged according to an arbitrary or preconceived pattern, but should be suggested by the subjects themselves. How best in practice to set about subject indexing in general and classifying in particular will be dealt with later (XII a, b). It will usually be found, however, that most specific subjects can be grouped under more general heads, but that a number must remain uncategorised in their original alphabetical positions.

If space allows, it is obviously desirable to have cross-references from every specific subject to the group heading under which it is situated. They should be in the form

Abbeys see under Religious houses

But when economy is essential most of these cross-references may be omitted, provided that there is a warning note at the beginning of the index reading: 'Most subjects are arranged in groups, the principal groups being under the headings: . . .' It is still, of course, necessary to have cross-references from specific subjects to smaller group headings excluded from the warning note; and '<i>see also</i>' cross-references berween any groups which have overlapping interests, for example between 'Customs dues' or 'Customs and Excise' and 'Taxation', and even sometimes between two specific subheadings in different groups.

The necessity for '<i>see also</i>' cross-references may at first sight suggest that the classification has been inadequately carried out, but in fact it is the inevitable result of avoiding enormous and complicated groupings. For many kinds of records the heading 'Agriculture' would produce too large and complex an entry. It is then better to have a few smaller, although still quite lengthy, entries headed 'Crops', 'Farm equipment', 'Livestock', and so on. 'Economic affairs' and 'Legal matters' are two other groupings which may often prove to be too general for the same reason. As a general rule, the nearer to the main topic or interest of the text the subjects are, the less general should their groupings be. Thus 'Legal matters' would be an absurd heading in a Subject Index to a volume of <i>Curia Regis Rolls</i>. The resulting entry would stretch to more than half the length of the index. A number of smaller groups of subjects, relating to more specific aspects of the law, have to be made instead. 'Agriculture', by contrast, is a perfectly manageable category in the <i>Curia Regis Rolls</i>, although it would be far too general for the <i>Calendar of Inquisitions Miscellaneous</i>.

(c) *Headings*

There will often be a number of different words or phrases under which a subject, or a group of subjects, could be indexed. The indexer must decide in each case under which heading searchers will be most likely to look for it. In indexes to record publications the more technical type of heading is usually preferable to its popular synonyms. Users of Subject Indexes may be expected to know the technical vocabulary and to prefer its greater precision. Group headings should never be vague or imprecise, but merely wider in scope than their subheadings.

Whatever headings are chosen, there should be cross-references from all reasonable synonyms, particularly from those used in the text, except that there need not be cross-references, if space is short, to those main group headings which are specifically mentioned in the prefatory note to the index. There may also be a few simple entries with only a few references for which it is as brief, and more useful, to repeat the references under each or every synonym as to cross-refer. But when the references are numerous or, especially, when there are subheadings or modifications, one heading only should form the entry, with cross-references from any synonyms which might reasonably be looked up. Thus if there are entries for 'Livestock' and 'Diseases', it is useful to have the cross-references

Animals *see* Livestock

Illnesses *see* Diseases

although there is no need to give the synonyms in brackets after the chosen headings. One crime which the indexer must avoid at all costs is to have some of the references to a subject under one heading and others under a synonym or synonyms. In that case there will certainly be no cross-reference between them, otherwise the crime would have been spotted and corrected; and the searcher will almost certainly miss some of his references.

Most antonyms should also appear in Subject Indexes only as cross-references to the headings of which they are the exact opposites, all the subentries being grouped under the positive word and rephrased in a negative form when necessary. For example, there should, where relevant, be a cross-reference

Divorce *see* Marriage

with all the references under 'Marriage'. The alternative often involves either repetition of subentries or the dispersal of cognate matters under the two heads.

It is sometimes difficult to decide whether a subject heading or subheading should be in the singular or the plural. The most important thing is to have a consistent practice, and it is therefore recommended that the plural form be used throughout the index. It does not matter that some of the references will be to occurrences of the subject in the singular: the user will not expect every reference under the heading 'Seals' to lead to mentions of more than one seal. By contrast, the singular heading makes the wording of subentries concerning the subject in the plural either circumlocutory or misleading. It follows from the recommendation of the plural that there should never be two headings for the same subject, one in the singular and the other in the plural, even if they are next to each other, which would not always be so; while the heading 'Seal(s)' to cover both forms is clumsy and unnecessary.

The simpler the heading the better, and one-word headings are ideal, but unfortunately they are not always possible, especially for group headings. Some groups are formed by bringing together two, or occasionally even more, closely related subjects, which greatly gain from association. They often demand a compound heading. If, for example, one unites matters relating to fish and matters relating to fishing, which it would usually be wise to do, a composite heading 'Fish and Fishing' is necessary. The component elements of such headings will rarely be alphabetically adjacent, as 'Fish' and 'Fishing' might well be. When they are not, there should be cross-references from the second and any subsequent elements, for example

Plans *see* Maps and Plans

unless the heading is one of those listed in the note to the index. A number of such groupings, made desirable because the component parts overlap, come readily to mind as suitable for many record publications: 'Clergy and Religious'; 'Customs and Services'; 'Food and Drink'; 'Forests and Woods'; 'Markets and Fairs'; 'Officials and Servants'; 'Weapons and Armour'; and so on. The word to appear first should be the more important, which will usually be the one upon which greater emphasis is placed, as in the examples just cited. Incidentally, such composite entries often necessitate a different type of subentry which is discussed later (V f).

So far we have considered only simple headings, consisting of a single noun, and those compound headings which consist of two or three nouns linked by the word 'and'. Other forms of compound heading are equally legitimate, although they should never run to more than a few words. Such phrased headings have to be considered in order to decide in each case which of the words is the really significant one—the word which users would be most likely to turn to. It is usually the most specific word. Sometimes it will be the first one, in which case the phrase will form the heading in its natural order, as with 'Building materials', 'Household articles', 'Civil Service' and 'Home Office'. Nobody would think of looking for any of these subjects under their second words, and so no cross-references are required from them. It follows from these examples that there is no need to change the order of the words merely because the first word is an adjective or participle, provided that it is the significant and specific word. 'Black Death' is a good subject heading. No cross-reference from 'Death' is necessary. To invert the words and index under 'Death, Black', merely to bring the noun to the beginning, would be absurd: the entry would be lost. Only conjunctions and articles can be completely ruled out as possible key words, being always transposed to the end. Indeed, articles should only be used in headings and subheadings when they are in titles of books, pamphlets and papers, and names of ships and taverns; for example

Figaro, Le, 67
North Briton, The, 521

Prepositions should be the first words of headings only when they are the first words of titles of books.

Articles are not the only words in headings which require transposition. Whenever the significant word is not the first in the natural order, the heading must be inverted to bring it to the beginning as the key word. Thus 'Administration of Justice' would be an inadequate heading. 'Justice' is the specific word and must be the key word. The heading should therefore be 'Justice, administration of', with no cross-reference.

There will, however, always be some headings in which two or more words are of equal, or nearly equal, significance. 'Licences for the alienation of lands in mortmain' is a perfectly good heading, but there should be corresponding entries beginning 'Alienations', 'Lands' and 'Mortmain', either with all the references repeated under them or with cross-references to the natural order. The Conspiracy to Murder Bill is more complicated. Obviously it should be indexed in its natural order under 'C', with the article omitted, and also under either 'Bills' or a more general heading such as 'Parliament', again in its natural order. But it should also appear under 'Murder' or the 'murder' subentry of 'Felony'. The difficulty here is that the index heading or subheading 'Murder' is a noun, not a verb. It would therefore be wrong for our modification to read

bill concerning conspiracy to, 156

It must be reworded, in order to fit the context grammatically

bill concerning conspiracy to commit,
156

The wording of subentries, however, is a separate subject which will have its own section (V f).

Just as persons should never be indexed merely in the form of initials if they can be identified (IV a), so should organizations normally be written in full for subject headings. They should only appear in the index by their initials if they so occur in the text, and even then the entry should merely take the form of a cross-reference to the full title. If, for example, the text mentions the I.R.A. thus, there should be index entries reading

I.R.A. see Irish Republican Army
Irish Republican Army (I.R.A.), 27, 96

Under the system of alphabetical arrangement recommended below (VII b) the first entry comes at the beginning of the letter 'I', only preceded by any other sets of initials whose second letters are before 'R' in the alphabet, and not just before Iran. The only exception to this rule for the treatment of initials of organizations is when the initials are far better known than the words for which they stand and can be pronounced as if they formed a single word, like UNESCO. These can be justifiably used as main index entries, with cross-references from the spelled-out versions. They should be indexed twice: first at the beginning of the relevant letters, and again in the positions they would occupy if they really were single words. Such abbreviations, unlike all other entry headings consisting of initials, do not need full stops after each letter, but it is clearer if they are printed in capitals rather than as ordinary words (e.g. Unesco) as is sometimes done.

(d) *Homonyms*

Homonymous subject headings should be avoided whenever possible. This can be done by using synonyms or by joining the homonyms with other words to form compound entries which are unambiguous. Thus instead of three different entries all headed 'Customs' there could well be the following

Customs and Services
Customs dues
Laws and Customs

and instead of two headed 'Fines'

Final concords
Fines and Amercements

When the use of homonyms is unavoidable, they should be defined in round brackets, as in the following examples

Liberties (geographical areas)
Liberties (privileges)
Wards (administrative areas)
Wards (feudal)

It is essential to repeat the homonymous headings whenever they change their meaning, and unforgivable to conflate or in any way confuse the subentries of one of them with those of another.

Homonymous subject headings should be arranged alphabetically by the words of descriptions in brackets, with any organization, book or journal coming last of all. A series of entries might run

Stocks (financial), 79, 102
Stocks (horticulture), 39
Stocks (punitive), 177
Stocks, 152

(the last being an imaginary journal more likely in real life to have some such title as *The Stocks and Shares Weekly*). This particular sequence is, of course, unlikely to occur in any index to a record publication. Even if the three varieties of stocks all occurred in the text, some, if not all, would certainly be grouped with cognate subjects under more general headings, the only entries under 'S' perhaps being

Stocks *see* Finance; Flowers; Punish-
ments
Stocks, 152

If, in our unlikely series of homonymous entries, 'Stocks (financial)' were enlarged to 'Stocks and Shares', the order of entries would be

Stocks (horticulture), 39
Stocks (punitive), 177
Stocks, 152
Stocks and Shares, 79, 102

because the words in brackets are not part of the headings and the single word 'Stocks' takes precedence alphabetically over a composite heading beginning with that word.

(e) *Persons, Places and Subjects*

It sometimes appears from the number of cross-references that a large amount of the Subject Index is the result of indexing not the text but the Index of Persons and Places. Castles, woods, etc., which appear as subentries under the relevant places, and offices, which should appear either under places or after the names of their holders or in both entries, are subjects and should therefore be in the Subject Index also. Their subject entries are often oblique, as follows

Castles *see* Index of Persons and Places
under Arundel; Dover; Oswes-
try; Pevensey; Warwick

or, if there are also mentions of castles generally as well as of named castles,

Castles, 79, 123, 560. *See also* Index of
Persons and Places *under* Arundel; Dover; Oswestry; Warwick

Alternatively, such subjects can be indexed simply, by direct reference to the text, as in

Castles, 16, 62, 79, 123, 188, 197, 199,
314, 560

This is normally preferable. It takes up less space, it is therefore cheaper, and it is what the user wants. If he is interested in one particular castle he will turn first to the place in the Index of Persons and Places. The searcher who turns to the subject entry 'Castles' can be assumed to be interested in castles more generally, and it is exasperating for him to find that he is merely referred to a number of places among which his references are distributed. As a general rule, therefore, subject headings of this kind should be followed by numerical references, not cross-references, but the rule is subject to two qualifications. First, some subjects, such as manors and churches, are frequently so numerous that even to list their numerical references can take a dozen or more lines: to cross-refer to the individual manors or churches could take up several columns, and does in those, mainly pre-war, indexes which contain such entries. Both practices are undesirable in such cases, and

Manors, passim

is of relatively little value. The best that can be done is to begin the entry with

Manors see Index of Persons and Places
under particular places

and to follow this with as many modifications as are needed, each dealing with some aspect of the subject occurring in the text which is of a specifically 'subject' nature, for example

Manors see Index of Persons and Places
under particular places
chapels of, 346, 391
fortified buildings of, 317
laws and customs of, 287
moated, 54, 119

Such modifications would, of course, still appear if the first line contained numerical references, although there would be no need to repeat after the heading numbers for which there were modifications.

The other subjects of this kind whose headings are not necessarily followed by references are those of the great officers of state. As already stated in connection with peerages and bishoprics (IV m), whenever a particular officer is meant and can be identified the reference should be under his name; and because such references are often numerous they should not be repeated in the Subject Index, where the references should be confined to impersonal mentions of the office. Thus a typical subject entry for one of the great officers might begin

Chancellors, 16, 72, 98, 156, 332. See
also Index of Persons and Places
under Morton, John; Warham,
William; Wolsey, Thomas

Any necessary modifications would then follow. Lesser officials do not require cross-references to their names, but only numerical references. If the references are very numerous, as they will often be for vicars and rectors, a general direction to their parishes similar to that recommended for manors is all that can be given. A few officials figure only in the Subject Index. The treasurer and barons of the Exchequer, for example, warrant only a subject entry—under 'Exchequer', with cross-references from 'Treasurers' and 'Barons'.

(f) Subheadings and Modifications: Wording

Although most of the examples given in this section are of subject entries, since their wording presents the most acute problems, the principles discussed are equally applicable to persons and places, particularly to the subject modifications of places, and so a few examples of these are also provided.

The first rule for subheadings and modifications, as indeed for subject headings, is that they should be specific, self-explanatory and unambiguous. The second is that they should be as brief as possible, although not so brief as to create ambiguity or vagueness. It is in the modifications of subject entries that the temptation to rewrite the text is at its strongest. The temptation to give all the details in the following modification is almost overwhelming

> Priors, 78, 922
>> murdered by blow to head from
>> earthen pot during quarrel with
>> friars while drinking, 116

But it must be resisted. Indexes with such modifications make fascinating reading, but that is not the purpose. References to the above event will, of course, be given under entries such as 'Murder' or 'Felony', 'Household articles' and 'Friars', but under 'Priors' all that is required is 'murdered', or 'murder of' if that form is preferred.

Words can be saved in a number of other ways. One is by omitting all articles, definite and indefinite, except for those which are parts of personal and place names, of titles of books and journals, and of names of ships and taverns. Another saving is to avoid, whenever possible, repeating the heading or subheading in modifications. Indeed, the whole purpose of modifications being to modify the preceding heading or subheading, the latter can be understood as having to be read with them. A comma is normally used to indicate the point at which the heading or subheading (the word or words represented by the indentation) must be inserted into the modification. Thus in the entry

> Ships, 57, 99, 122
>> crews of, murdered, 111

the second line is to be understood as 'crews of ships murdered'. This practice is recommended here. Nevertheless, despite its neatness and clarity, there are still those who argue strongly for the repetition of headings and subheadings in all modifications, while others advocate that they be represented by a dash or, in the case of single-word headings, by the initial letter.

Some indexers greatly prefer 'murder of' to 'murdered' in examples such as the last and for the abbreviated modification under 'Priors', and try to arrange that for all modifications the wording should be such that the last word, normally a preposition, relates specifically to the main heading, last subheading or even, in more complex cases, to the previous modification. Such 'rounded' modifications—perhaps 'twisted back' would be a better description—sound complete and, more important, are always immediately understandable and unambiguous. The same cannot be said for all single-word modifications, which often fail to convey their exact relationship with the heading or subheading or with a previous modification. There are, however, three kinds of subject entry which do not allow of 'rounded' modifications. One is the paragraphed entry, which is discussed in detail elsewhere (XI d). The sole merit of paragraphing is that it saves space, and it is therefore logical that yet more space should be saved by making all subentries as concise as possible. Moreover, in large paragraphs it would be merely confusing to have every subheading and modification referring back in a very exact way to the main heading. Also inappropriate for 'rounded' modifications are the composite entry with a compound heading such as 'Fish and Fishing', and the entry with a fairly general heading such as 'Agriculture' or 'Economic affairs': entries whose headings will rarely be followed by direct references and which will usually stand on a line by themselves (see XI f). Their subentries need be no briefer than the 'rounded' ones. The only difference is that they are complete in themselves instead of, in effect, incorporating the main heading.

Such an entry might run

> AGRICULTURE
>> barley, sowing of, 321
>> carts, with four oxen, 628
>> common of pasture, 626
>> corn, 32
>>> threshing of, 214
>> cultivation, prevention of, 658
>> harvesting, 114

The question here arises as to how internally consistent the wording of sub-headings and modifications should be, especially in the Subject Index. An index in which every entry is arranged in a paragraph can easily be kept consistent by pruning every subentry down to the minimum number of words. But most other indexes will contain some entries which allow the modifications to be 'twisted back' to connect with the headings, and others which do not. Does this mean that the wording of all modifications should be ordered as those of the latter entries must be: that the 'rounding' of modifications should be avoided in all cases because it cannot be applied in every one? Few users will read through entry after entry and then be worried by such a minor inconsistency. There should, of course, be as much consistency as possible within each entry, and there is usually no reason why this consistency should not be complete. Otherwise common sense must determine exactly which ordering is appropriate in each case.

The indexer must ensure that a modification which is 'twisted back' cannot be used, by indentation, to run on to further words in a subsequent modification. Thus one should never have entries in the form

> Attorneys, 305, 499, 1601
>> appointments of, 1430, 1973
>>> on account of pregnancy, 1711
>> sons as, 1452
>> wives as, 820
> Corpses, 67
>> removal of, 129
>> clothing from, 233

The relevant words must be repeated, the correct wording being

> Attorneys, 305, 499, 1601
>> appointments of, 1430, 1973
>>> on account of pregnancy, 1711
>> appointments of sons as, 1452
>> appointments of wives as, 820
> Corpses, 67
>> removal of, 129
>> removal of clothing from, 233

These entries are correct because, unlike the first versions, they associate the heading with the appropriate preposition in every modification.

The practices of three schools of indexers in this matter of the linking of modifications to headings and subheadings are not recommended. One advocates that every effort should be made to avoid ending a modification with a preposition, but otherwise approves of the 'twisted back' form. They would write

Edward V, king, murder of, in Tower,
55

instead of

Edward V, king, murder in Tower of,
55

This is a minor variation and a matter of individual taste. It is discouraged here because it can result in the inclusion of unnecessary words, such as 'in Tower' in the last example. But if it is thought desirable to include 'in Tower' anyway, the second version is still better as it has the practical advantage of containing one fewer break. Index entries should flow as naturally as possible, and punctuation should be kept to a minimum (see X a-c). Another school, arguing that it is unnecessary for modifications to consist, with headings or subheadings, of complete phrases, takes word-saving to the extreme of omitting the final preposition of modifications as being superfluous. They would render the last entry

Edward V, king, murder in Tower, 55

In less familiar contexts this could be ambiguous since either 'of' or 'by' might have been omitted. If the preposition is disliked, a slight rewording without increasing the number of words is more satisfactory. The example chosen could be amended to read

Edward V, king, murdered in Tower,
55

which, as already stated, is a perfectly satisfactory form of entry. The third school is strongly opposed both to the final preposition and to the form of modification which produces it. They would index the same passage as

Edward V, king, his murder in Tower,
55

They also, wherever possible, make use of the present tense, as in

Edward IV, king, dies, 12

rather than

Edward IV, king, death of, 12

This form of wording is more useful for persons than for places or subjects. It is quite suitable for paragraphed entries, particularly in General Indexes in which the major characters have entries of some length (see VI a). But it is not recommended for entries whose modifications all begin on separate lines.

It is not only the final word of modifications which is important. The first word is even more so. There are two extreme views about what the first word should be. Some indexers leave all modifications in their natural order, whereas others ensure that they all begin with their most significant word by inverting all those in which that word does not naturally come first. Experience alone can lead the indexer to that happy mean which is here recommended. Whenever possible the most significant word should come first, and simple inversion to ensure that it does is perfectly in order. Such words are frequently ones which in many indexes, often indeed in the same index, themselves constitute entry headings or subheadings, or their key words, as in our earlier example

Priors, murder of, 116

One should soon become skilled in so phrasing modifications that the significant word comes first, while avoiding those cumbersome convolutions and distortions of order which disfigure some indexes. But in concentrating on these two things—giving priority to the significant word and ensuring that the words flow naturally—it is easy to separate two words which should be closely associated or to fail to appreciate that there are two modifications and not just one. Thus

> Works, 17, 22
>   autumn, 69
>   villeins' refusal to perform boon, 79

should read

> Works, 17, 22
>   autumn, 69
>   boon, villeins' refusal to perform, 79

The failure to appreciate that there are really two modifications is more likely when there are no references to the first modification alone and no other modifications of it: in our example, no mention of boon works in any other context.

The subentries of persons and places are normally brief and of such a nature that they are unlikely to be introduced by any word other than the significant one: the forename of a relative or the title of an office in the case of persons; a word such as 'abbey', 'battle', 'church' or 'inquisition' under places. But with some subject entries it is impossible to avoid beginning a modification with a preposition or even a conjunction. Some indexers try to avoid this by inversion, as follows

> Murders, 27, 98
>   abbots, of, 32
>   constables, of, 526-7
>   madmen, by, 336

but this is too unnatural and disjointed. In such cases the prepositions must introduce the significant words, to give the reading

> Murders, 27, 98
>   by madmen, 336
>   of abbots, 32
>   of constables, 526-7

(g) Subheadings and Modifications: Alphabetical Order

We have just noted that the subentries of persons and places are always introduced by significant words. One can be fairly confident that they are the words for which searchers will look, and their alphabetical arrangement presents no difficulties. Subject entries are more complicated. We have seen that their modifications can usually be so worded or inverted that the significant word comes first, in which case they should be arranged in strict alphabetical order under the main heading, or in a series of separate alphabets under the various subheadings, which should themselves be in alphabetical order. There are four exceptions to this rule. One is when there are a number of modifications of the main heading and also a number of specific subheadings. They should not be merged into a single alphabetical sequence like the following

> Crops, 79, 382, 594
>   barley, 67, 82
>   corn, 1, 9, 17, 63, 194, 288, 400
>   destroyed by floods, 694
>   destroyed by Scots, 74, 132
>   eaten by cattle, 399
>   maslin, 760

Crops (*contd*)
    oats, 5, 12, 19, 341
    peas, 77, 195, 372
    rye, 118, 332, 376
    sown in spring, 2, 340
    sown in winter, 555
    tithes of, *q.v.*
    trampled by cattle, 56
    unlawfully removed, 292, 396
    wheat, 17-19, 21, 66, 144, 319, 422,
       596

It is both clearer and more useful to have the modifications of the heading all together at the beginning, followed by the subheadings, each forming their own alphabet, as follows

Crops, 79, 382, 594
    destroyed by floods, 694
    destroyed by Scots, 74, 132
    eaten by cattle, 399
    sown in spring, 2, 340
    sown in winter, 555
    tithes of, *q.v.*
    trampled by cattle, 56
    unlawfully removed, 292, 396
    types of
        barley, 67, 82
        corn, 1, 9, 17, 63, 194, 288, 400
        maslin, 760
        oats, 5, 12, 19, 341
        peas, 77, 195, 372
        rye, 118, 332, 376
        wheat, 17-19, 21, 66, 144, 319,
           422, 596

Similar divisions will often be desirable for 'Clergy and Religious', 'Clothing', 'Customs and Services', 'Livestock', 'Officials and Servants', 'Records', 'Religious houses' and others. By contrast, such group entries as 'Building materials', 'Ecclesiastical articles', 'Furniture', 'Household articles', 'Occupations' and 'Weapons and Armour' will often, although not always, consist of nothing but specific items and will therefore merely have these in alphabetical order under the heading, beginning, for example, thus

Occupations
    baker, 532
    barber, 67
    brewer, 233
    butcher, 5, 82, 397

The second exception to the rule for a single alphabetical sequence is similar. When there are many parts of some concrete subject, such as the tackle of ships, they are also best arranged in their own sequence after all the more general modifications of 'Ships'. They can be introduced by some term such as 'parts of' or 'tackle of' in lieu of 'types of' in our 'Crops' example. Thirdly, named items should also be separately alphabetised. Inns and, once again, ships are often named. Indeed, the entry 'Ships' is unique in that it may well contain all three exceptions, when it will have to be arranged in four separate alphabets as follows

Ships, arrested, 132, 226, 350
    crews of, attacked and wounded, 355
    freighted outside the staple, 608
    sunk, 618
    wrecked upon coasts, 356, 448
    named
        Cholseyesbarge, 355
        Christofre, le, 455
        Elynore, 572
        Gabriell, la, 376
        Gracedieu, la, 536
        James, le, 536
        Marie Knyght, la, 376
        Notre Dame, 552
        Sancta Maria, 554
        Trinite, la, (two ships), 276, 594
    tackle of
        anchors, 270, 355, 455
        bowsprits, 455
        cables, 270, 355, 375
        hawsers, 455
        masts, 455, 553-4
        oars, 455, 618
        ropes, 618
        sails, 355, 618
    types of
        balingers, 213, 226-7, 276
        barges, 196, 213, 276, 619-20
        carracks, 355-6, 375, 553-4
        crayers, 270
        gondolas, 356
        picards, 554
        skiffs, 565
        trows, 474

There is a case for having the named ships at the very end in that their association with the heading is slightly less direct than is that of the items of the other two subdivisions. The fact that 'named', 'tackle' and 'types' would not then be in alphabetical order is not important. But if the items in all three subdivisions had been merged with the earlier modifications into one alphabet the result would have been much less clear. It would, of course, have been impossibly confusing if the entry had been in the form of a paragraph. However short the entries, modifications of headings should always come before any subheadings in indexes arranged in paragraphs.

    Two small points arise from our 'Ships' example, which may be conveniently dealt with before we move on to the fourth exception. One concerns the two ships named *la Trinite*. It will be very seldom that two ships of the same name cannot be distinguished in some way in the index: by their port, nationality, owner or master, when they should be so indexed, as

> *Elynore*, of Denmark, 572
> *Elynore*, of Norway, 307
> *Notre Dame* of La Rochelle, 552
> *Notre Dame* of Toulouse, 16
> *Trinite, la*, John Helston master,
>   594
> *Trinite, la*, John Morgan master,
>   276

Only when such information is not available does one have to indicate in brackets that more than one ship is referred to, as with our *la Trinite*. (For more on this indexing convention see IV n; X g.) Incidentally, masters and owners of ships should be so described in the Index of Persons and Places, just as if they were office holders, while it is also useful to have a subentry 'ships of' under all relevant foreign countries, although without naming the ships, and those which are described as belonging to particular ports should be fully indexed under those ports, for example

> Rochelle, La, (la Rochell), [dep. Cha-
>   rente Maritime], France, ship
> *Notre Dame* of, 552

unless the ships of any port are numerous, when the following entry is adequate

> Rochelle, La, (la Rochell), [dep. Cha-
>   rente Maritime], France, ships
> *(named)* of, 62, 159, 443, 552,
>   617

The second point concerns the inversion of the article to bring the significant word of the ships' names to the beginning. It would be possible in such an entry to keep the article at the beginning and still alphabetise by the next word. But the article must never determine the alphabetical order, otherwise in our example well over half the ships would come under 'le' or 'la'. It is better to invert because it makes the alphabetical arrangement absolutely clear and because it is consistent with what has already been recommended (V c, d) for books, pamphlets, etc., whether they constitute main headings or subheadings.

The fourth exception to the rule for strict alphabetical order of modifications is when there are a number of modifications which are identical except for certain numbers or values mentioned in them. The shortcomings of an alphabetical arrangement (column on the left) as compared with a numerical one (on the right) are illustrated in the following example

Juries, intimidation of, 79	Juries, intimidation of, 79
of eight men, 24	of six men, 79
of six men, 79	of eight men, 24
of thirty-six men, 8	of twelve men, 9, 26
of twelve men, 9, 26	of twenty men, 30
of twenty men, 30	of twenty-four men, 6, 58
of twenty-eight men, 76	of twenty-eight men, 76
of twenty-four men, 6, 58	of thirty-six men, 8

Nothing is gained by strict alphabetical order in such cases, and the numerical arrangement is obviously sensible, although such modifications are usually among others in a longer entry which will be in alphabetical order and among which the numerically arranged ones will jointly occupy their correct alphabetical position.

We saw in the last section (V f) that it is sometimes necessary for the first word of a modification of a subject entry to be a preposition. This raises the question as to whether the preposition should be used or disregarded for determining the alphabetical position of the modification within the entry. If all prepositions are disregarded and the next significant word is used to determine the order, the following simple entry would run as in the column on the left, compared with the order on the right where the prepositions are used in alphabetising

Murders, 27, 98, 616	Murders, 27, 98, 616
of abbots, 32	by butchers, 16
in barns, 274	by highwaymen, 6, 527
of bishops, 336	by madmen, 336
by butchers, 16	by surgeons, 58
with clubs, 58, 412	in barns, 274
of constables, 526-7	in prison, 333
with daggers, 32	in ships, 17, 449
when drunk, 526	in taverns, 2, 98
by highwaymen, 6, 527	of abbots, 32
with knives, 39, 122	of bishops, 336
by madmen, 336	of constables, 526-7
with poison, 299	of sheriffs, 542
in prison, 333	when drunk, 526
of sheriffs, 542	with clubs, 58, 412
in ships, 17, 449	with daggers, 32
by surgeons, 58	with knives, 39, 122
in taverns, 2, 98	with poison, 299

Both arrangements are commonly encountered, and some indexers who alphabetise by significant words use a capital for the first letter of such words. The result is ugly, and especially inappropriate in General Indexes in which the key word of the main heading is in the lower case (see VI a). It is hardly preferable to the inversion of the preposition (see V f). But space need not be spent in discussing such practices. It is hoped that the superior merits of the arrangement in the right-hand column will be self evident. A number of useful sub-groups have formed naturally without any need of subheadings and double indentation, whereas the arrangement by significant words is virtually a random arrangement so far as the sense of the modifications is concerned. What this means is that the prepositions in this example, as very often, are by no means insignificant words and certainly need not be discounted as being unworthy of determining alphabetical positions. This usefully reinforces the rule, which might otherwise have been submerged by the necessarily lengthy consideration of its exceptions, that the great majority of subject entries are internally arranged in strict alphabetical order.

CHAPTER VI

GENERAL AND SPECIAL INDEXES

(a) *General Indexes*

It is rarely possible to justify having more than one index to a secondary work, for which reason nearly every authority on indexing has strongly advocated a single General Index for every book. In the case of record publications, however, the arguments for a General Index and those for two, or occasionally more, indexes are more evenly matched. On the one hand, if there is more than one index the hasty searcher sometimes misses his entry by neglecting to notice the fact and looking only in the wrong one; and if it is thought desirable to have a substantial number of cross-references between subject entries and persons and places, a General Index makes them slightly shorter and easier to pursue. But if there are few or no cross-references of that nature, and we have already seen that they should be kept to a minimum (V e), it is often better to have the subjects in a separate index. They are normally far fewer in number than the persons and places, and in a General Index the small, individually indexed subjects can easily be lost to sight, while the large grouped subject entries with their subheadings and modifications appear almost as a disruption of the even course of the basic alphabetical arrangement. In a relatively short Subject Index the major subject groupings and also the general nature of the subject entries are much more readily apparent than if dispersed among a large number of persons and places.

Such are the general arguments, but the decision as between a General Index and separating the subjects should always depend upon the nature of the records in every particular case. In many kinds of records the connection between the persons and places and most of the subjects is largely adventitious. For example, a considerable number of the important subjects in the Chancery classes of Inquisitions *post mortem* and Miscellaneous Inquisitions are economic ones, and those in the Curia Regis Rolls are, naturally, mainly legal. The published volumes of these records have been given separate Subject Indexes because for most searchers interested in these topics the particular persons and places involved in them are largely immaterial, while those who follow up the references to a person or place will find the subject context anyway.

By contrast, there are other classes of documents in which the more important persons and places are virtually subjects, or at least are inextricably intertwined with the most central subjects. The best examples are the main series of State Papers (Domestic, Foreign and Colonial), in which the most important subjects are the events of the periods covered, which are invariably closely associated with some of the persons and places. Hence the printed calendars of these records have General Indexes.

The majority of entries in a General Index will always consist of persons and places which are identical in their form to the corresponding entries in any separate Index of Persons and Places. The rest are of two kinds: normal subject entries, consisting of individual subjects and of subject groups; and the important persons and places, each of which will have a fair number of subentries of a subject nature. The problem with the first of these—the individual subject entries, which are always very few compared with the persons and places—is how to get them to stand out. The most effective as well as the simplest solution is to print their headings entirely in the lower case, except for those words which always command an initial capital.[1] Surprisingly, this small alteration serves to distinguish them quite clearly from the persons and places. The group entries can also be lost, but for another reason: not because they are too insignificant to be readily picked out, but because in a General Index it is very difficult to locate some of them unless every guidance is given to the headings used. Every subject group must therefore be listed in the prefatory note to the index, and there must also be full cross-references from the normal alphabetical positions of all sub-headings to the group headings, as well as from all reasonable synonyms. It may also be useful to have the group headings printed entirely in small capitals with each heading standing on a line of its own (see XI f). Only in these ways can such subjects be prevented from being submerged among the persons and places.

The last-mentioned typographical device—small capitals—may also be thought to be useful for the headings of those central persons and places under which the other subject entries appear as subheadings and modifications. Under each person and place the subentries can be set out alphabetically in the normal way, inverted or reworded as necessary to bring the significant word to the beginning. Alternatively, they can be arranged either chronologically or, what usually amounts to almost the same thing, in the numerical order of their first references.

While it is true that the last system—arrangement in numerical order of references—results in the subentries being in approximate chronological order, if the purpose is to achieve chronological order it is much preferable, if slightly more arduous, to do it properly. Some indexers even apply this system to all entries in all types of index, and not just to the important persons and places in General Indexes. Their justification is that, apart from the fact that it produces a rough and ready chronological arrangement, the book order is especially useful for those who are interested in all the references. But, carried to its logical conclusion, this is virtually an argument for having no subentries at all. Also, of course, it is only the first reference of each which is in book order.

Arrangement by references is therefore to be discouraged in all circumstances, but a chronological arrangement is often particularly well suited to the complex persons and places entries when the records relate to the main stream of a country's history. In long entries it is sometimes helpful to insert dates in brackets before the references: in round brackets if they are obtained from the text, and in square ones if from elsewhere. But they should only be included if they are definite, and there is no need to go beyond the basic standard works of reference to discover them. A complication is that there are often a few sub-entries of a more general nature relating to the same persons and places, which do not permit of chronological treatment. The best thing is to put them first in alphabetical order before the main chronological sequence of subentries. Such hybrid entries are not ideal and require a clear explanation in a prefatory note, as, indeed, does any arrangement of subentries other than a purely alphabetical one. If the hybrid entries become numerous it may well be that it is preferable to revert to a strictly alphabetical arrangement.

The tendency for entries to become over-large, already mentioned in connection with grouped subject entries (V b), is even stronger in the case of persons and places with subject modifications. It must always be resisted. As a general rule, the closer the person or place to the main interest of the records, the more essential

[1] In separate Subject Indexes, however, the key word of every entry should begin with a capital letter.

it is to break the entry up, making what would otherwise be the major subentries into main entries and distributing them about the index in their correct alphabetical positions, although there will always remain a residue of modifications under the person or place as well as cross-references to the items removed. Unless this dispersal is carried out, most of the subject matter of some volumes would have to be sought under a very few persons and places, and individual items would almost certainly be found only with difficulty. It is sufficient merely to suggest the impossibly long entries and multiplicity of subheadings and modifications which would result if every subject concerning the king in the *Calendar of State Papers, Domestic Series, James II*, were grouped under the heading 'James II, king', or if every mention of the bishop in a transcript of his register were to be indexed under his name.

One final complication encountered in General Indexes concerns homonymous headings. We have already seen how homonymous place names should be arranged (III n), how persons having surnames identical to place names should be ordered in relation to the places (*ibid.*), and how homonymous subject headings and titles of organizations, books and journals should be arranged among themselves (V d). General Indexes, however, can contain them all, and in them the order of homonymous headings is places, persons, subjects and titles of organizations and books. Thus a series of entries might run

Stocks, The, in Seend [in Melksham],
    Wilts, 288
Stocks, John, 27
    William, 390
stocks (financial), 79, 102
stocks (horticulture), 39
stocks (punitive), 177
Stocks, 152

(b) *Special Indexes*

With the exception of volumes which demand General Indexes, record publications are best served by having two: an Index of Persons and Places and an Index of Subjects; and the preceding chapters have been written on the assumption that that will be the normal pattern. But there is one situation in which it is not merely justifiable but positively desirable to have three indexes, persons being separated from places. That is when the records all, or nearly all, relate to a single county, and the practice is therefore best suited to the publications of county record societies. In a separate Index of Places much space can be saved by giving the name of a county only for those few places in other counties which happen to be mentioned in the text, always provided, of course, that there is a note at the beginning of the index stating that all other places are in the county to which the documents relate. Yet more space can be saved by the use of the abbreviations 'N', 'S', 'E' and 'W' in place names distinguished by the words North, South, East and West. Neither economy can so easily be made in a single Index of Persons and Places, where the use of abbreviations for the points of the compass can be confused with personal initials, especially if no county is given; and where it is the inclusion of the name of the county after the place name which immediately distinguishes place names from surnames, although there are fortunately very few place names like Mavis Enderby, Edith Weston and Rose Maund (indexed as Enderby, Mavis; Weston, Edith; and Maund, Rose) which might cause more than momentary confusion. With the exception of volumes devoted to one county, record publications should have either a single Index of Persons and Places and a Subject Index, or, for the kind of records described in the last section, a General Index. It is only necessary to recall to mind archbishops of Canterbury and earls of Arundel, as examples of the point that the distinction between persons and places entries is not absolute, to justify this recommendation.

Just occasionally it is possible to allow a special index in addition to the normal one or two: an index of cases or statutes for certain legal records, of trades in records of an economic nature, of field names in agricultural ones or in rentals and surveys and similar documents, and perhaps of forenames or unusual words in very early records. If such a special index is included it is essential to give clear warnings of this both in a note at the beginning of the index, usually the Subject or General Index, in which the items would otherwise appear and also by means of cross-references from any relevant main headings at the appropriate points within that index. Special indexes can only be justified if their individual items are so numerous that they would completely upset the balance of the Subject or General Index, and if they relate to a subject which is peculiarly important in the records in the text or in their period. They should never be compiled unless these two conditions obtain.

CHAPTER VII

WORDING AND ALPHABETICAL ORDER

The purpose of this chapter is to bring together the various points already made in connection with these cognate subjects before we turn, in the remaining chapters, to the more technical aspects of indexing.

(a) *Wording*
If this book had been written only ten years ago, it would have been necessary to begin this section with an impassioned plea that all indexes be written in English, but the use of Latin seems now, at last, to have died out.[1] Our first rule concerning wording is that all headings, subheadings and modifications should be specific, unambiguous and self-explanatory. The second rule is that as few words as possible should be used, although never so few as to cause ambiguity or imprecision. In order to save words, articles should be omitted except those which are integral parts of personal and place names, of titles of books and journals, and of names of ships and inns; and indentation should be used instead of repeating headings, subheadings and modifications. Wherever possible, modifications should be of the 'rounded' variety, relating directly to the heading or the previous subheading or modification, although a different type of wording is necessary in paragraphed entries and for those composite and more general headings which stand on a line of their own. It does not matter that both types of modification should appear in the same index: that the majority should, in effect, be understood to incorporate the heading, while the rest are complete in themselves. (For the expanded treatment of the points in this paragraph see V f.)

The headings of persons and places entries choose themselves, but those of subject entries present greater difficulties. A technical heading is preferable to a more popular one, and a specific to a more general one. Headings which consist of more than one word often need to be inverted to bring the most significant word, which is usually the most specific one, to the beginning to serve as the key word. Most key words are nouns, but one must not automatically change the natural order to avoid other parts of speech. Some adjectives and participles are correctly used as key words when they are the first words of well known phrases and are also the most specific words in them. Only conjunctions and articles are never key words, being always transposed to the end, while prepositions are so used only if they are the first words of titles (see V c). Subheadings and modifications should also begin with their most significant and specific words wherever possible. It should always be possible in modifications of persons and places, but in some subject entries it is impossible to avoid beginning certain modifications with prepositions or even conjunctions, often with useful results (see V f, g).

It has been emphasised more than once that a minimum number of words should be used for index entries. But there are two methods of saving space which are not recommended. One is the use of abbreviations other than those already recommended. Recognizable abbreviations of English counties

---

[1] In the 1960s the Pipe Roll Society ceased to use Latin throughout its indexes and thus fell into line with all other record publishing societies.

can always be used after the names of places situated within them (see
III h); common personal styles can always be abbreviated in the normal way to
Dr, Mrs, etc. (IV k); and if space is very short frequently occurring forenames
can be shortened, 'sen' and 'jun' can be used for 'the elder' and 'the younger',
and, most extreme measure of all, close relationships can be indicated by 'd', 's'
and 'w' for 'daughter', 'son' and 'wife', while 'j' and 'w' can be used for 'juror' or
'justice' and 'witness' if such persons are numerous in a particular volume
(IV k, m). Any of these abbreviations used, other than those of counties and
personal styles, must be defined at the beginning of the index. Organizations
should only be indexed by their initials if they so appear in the text, and even
then the entry should merely take the form of a cross-reference to the full title
(V c).

   The other saving of space to be avoided is by the use of figures. They should
always be spelled out, especially when they immediately precede the references,
with which they can otherwise get confused, or if they introduce a modification.
They should never be the key words of entries, unless they are the first words
of titles in which case they must be written in full. Dates would be too cumbersome if spelled out, but when a date comes immediately before the references
it should be in brackets (see IV m; XI i).

(b) *Alphabetical Order: General*
Much of this subject has inevitably been anticipated in previous chapters and
will therefore only be summarised here. But first it is necessary to consider
which of the two methods of alphabetising should be applied to indexes to
record publications. One is the 'word-by-word' method, otherwise known as
'nothing before something', whereby the index entries are alphabetised primarily
by the first word of each heading, the second word being used only when there
are two or more entries with the same first word, the third word being used on
those rare occasions when entries have their first two words in common, and
so on up to the first comma. The other is variously described as the 'letter-by-
letter', the 'all-through' and the 'something-before-nothing' method, and, as
these descriptions suggest, its basis is to ignore the division into words and to
alphabetise by the whole heading up to the first comma as if all the letters ran
straight on without a break. At first it may seem not to be a very important matter
which method is chosen, but the positions of some entries can in a long index be
very different under one from what they would be under the other. The following simple example illustrates possible variations for a few entries, which might
amount to a difference of several pages in a sizable index.

Word by word	Letter by letter
New, John	New, John
New Forest	Newark
New Guinea	Newbury
New Hampshire	Newcastle upon Tyne
New Haven	New Forest
New Orleans	Newfoundland
New South Wales	New Guinea
New York	New Hampshire
New Zealand	New Haven
Newark	Newhaven
Newbury	New Orleans

Word by word (*contd*)	*Letter by letter* (*contd*)
Newcastle upon Tyne	New South Wales
Newfoundland	Newton, Isaac
Newhaven	New York
Newton, Isaac	New Zealand

Both usages have advantages and disadvantages, and they therefore seem to be almost equally popular with indexers. The chief advantage of the letter-by-letter system is that the position of entries whose headings are sometimes spelt as a single or hyphenated word and sometimes as two or more words is unaffected whichever form is chosen. A smaller one is that it seems right that New Haven and Newhaven should be adjacent rather than separated by eight entries in our example and by considerably more in the average index. New Haven, however, is untypical in that it is one of the relatively few place names whose qualifying word is not inverted for indexing (see III o). It is probably no accident that indexers of records relating to the New World seem to prefer letter by letter, while those concerned with British records, especially early ones, have tended to use word by word.

The word-by-word method can appear to result in two consecutive alphabetical sequences at times, as in our last example, but it is valuable in the Subject Index where it can prevent the dispersal of related entries, and even more valuable in the Index of Persons and Places where it ensures that all places with a common main element, for example Easton or Sutton, are adjacent whether or not they are qualified. It therefore seems all the more right that all uninverted places with the same adjective should come together, as do those beginning with 'New' in the word-by-word column of our last example.[2] But the benefits of word by word are most marked in the case of entries whose headings consist of initials. We have seen that initials should never form main headings if this can be avoided (V c), but some persons appear in the text only by their initials (IV a) and can only be indexed under them, while any organization which appears in the text by its initials should have a cross-reference from them in the index. We earlier used the I.R.A. to illustrate this point (V c). In an index arranged alphabetically letter by letter I.R.A. would appear in the second half of the letter 'I', possibly immediately before Iran, whereas under the word-by-word arrangement each initial is regarded as a separate word, as indeed it is, and so I.R.A. would be at the beginning of the letter 'I', only preceded by any other sets of initials whose second letters come earlier in the alphabet than 'R'. Such headings consisting solely of initials can be virtually lost if the index is alphabetised letter by letter, whereas they stand out if they are brought together at the beginning of each letter. Only those of the UNESCO type, which can be pronounced as though they were a single word and which can correctly be used as main headings (V c), might be looked for in the position they would occupy in the index if they really were one word. They should therefore be indexed twice under the word-by-word method.

Because of its superiority for initials and because all British places are indexed by their significant words (see III b), so that the occasional separation of a New

[2] It will be noticed that the surname New comes before the uninverted place names beginning with the word 'New'. This is not in breach of the rule given above (III n) that personal names follow homonymous place names or main elements thereof (whereby Newton Nottage and Newton, South, would have preceded Newton, Isaac, in our example), since 'New' is not a word of substance, so that New Forest must be treated as an entity and must follow the single-word heading 'New'.

Haven and a Newhaven is compensated for a hundredfold by the association of all British places with the same main word, word-by-word alphabetisation is recommended for all indexes to record publications. It is essential to use it consistently throughout the index, not only for main headings but also for sub-headings and modifications within each entry, so that the user can be sure where exactly to look for affected entries and subentries. There are, however, a few well recognized and accepted variations of the strict rule of the word-by-word method, most of which have been considered and illustrated in earlier chapters. They will merely be summarised here with reference in turn to places, persons, subjects and General Indexes.

(c) *Alphabetical Order: Places*

Homonymous places and places which have a common significant word must as a group occupy their correct alphabetical position in the index, but among themselves they should be arranged as follows: first, ecclesiastical areas, in the order province, diocese, archdeaconry, rural deanery; then any hundred, city, town, parish, township or manor; county; honor or liberty; province, state or other foreign administrative area; major physical features such as a forest, lake, mountain or river, arranged in alphabetical order thus; and finally any barony, duchy or dukedom, earldom or marquessate, again in that alphabetical order (for examples see III n). Homonymous places within the second group—hundreds, cities, towns, parishes, townships and manors—should be arranged among themselves according to the alphabetical order of their qualifying words, whether or not their order is inverted, any places having the main name un-qualified coming first. Examples have already been given (*ibid.*), but the following short sequence may usefully illustrate the principle again

> Stoke [in Acton], Ches, 194
> Stoke, East, Notts, 176
> Stoke, North, [in South Stoke], Lincs, 615
> Stoke Poges, Bucks, church, 516
> Stoke, South, Lincs, 224
>   Stoke, North, in, *q.v.*
> Stoke sub Hamdon, Som, 217
> Stoke, John, 25, 335
> Stokenham, Devon, Jackson of, *q.v.*

The word-by-word system of alphabetising is here breached by the disregarding of the fact that some places are in their natural order and others inverted, with the qualifying word separated by a comma. But it is a very satisfactory modifica-tion of the system, being both easy to apply and more useful than any alternative arrangement. By contrast, the following is the correct order for these two subject headings

> Defence, Ministry of, 16, 312
> Defence Bonds, 415

because according to the rule the comma in the first line renders the word 'Defence' alone primarily significant for alphabetising and it therefore precedes any multiple-word heading which begins with the same word and is not inverted.

It will be noticed that the word 'sub' in Stoke sub Hamdon is not disregarded for purposes of determining alphabetical order, and the rule is that no words should be ignored whatever their relative significance, as is explained more fully above (III n). Our earlier examples (*ibid.*) showed that when there are two or more places with the same unqualified name, or with the same qualification, their arrangement should be alphabetically by their counties, irrespective of the size of the places. But if there are two places with identical names in the same county and one is a parish or town and the other is smaller, they should be indexed in that order, any hundred coming first of all. Only when such places are of equal status need any descriptions supplied to distinguish them—usually hundreds in the case of parishes, and parishes for lesser places—be used to determine their order.

The obsolete forms of places given after the modern spelling in the main index entries should be in strict alphabetical order and never inverted, the alphabetical order being decided by the first word whether it is the main element or adjectival (see III c, d). Similarly when, in an index to a transcript, there is a single composite cross-reference from alphabetically adjacent obsolete forms to the modern spelling, the obsolete forms must again be in alphabetical order. The modifications of places are usually few and simple and should be arranged in strict alphabetical order, with three exceptions: cross-references to any persons described as of the places come at the very end, cross-references to places within them come next to last, and any named fields and other minor features form the modification or modifications immediately before that (III i). This is a sensible breach with strict alphabetical order. The alternatives are much inferior. If the three modifications were broken down into their individual parts and dispersed among the other modifications in alphabetical order, the entries would often be made much longer; and if they were kept intact but alphabetised by their first words, such modifications would appear at completely different points from entry to entry. Hence their consistent and useful position at the end. The persons, minor places and fields in these modifications are always to be listed in strict alphabetical order, the minor places being inverted if inverted in their own entries, but the field names never being inverted although any articles should be ignored in alphabetising them since their occurrence is very much a matter of chance. A slightly different arrangement is permissible for those places, usually London and one or two of the larger cities or boroughs, which have a large number of subentries. A single alphabetical sequence can be replaced by a system of grouped items, but the basic arrangement and the internal order within each grouping should still be strictly alphabetical, the group subheadings occupying their correct alphabetical positions among the other subentries (III k).

Two special kinds of place names and surnames are alphabetised in ways which might not be expected. Those beginning with the abbreviated word 'St' must be placed in the position they would occupy in the index if it were written in full as 'Saint', and equivalent foreign names should be treated likewise, being alphabetised as San, Santa, Sao, and so on. 'St' and its foreign equivalents are separate words for alphabetising by the word-by-word system (see IV i). Secondly, some foreign places with prefixes, and all post-medieval British surnames and certain foreign names which have prefixes are alphabetised as though the prefix and main name constituted a single word. Such names are therefore an exception to the normal rule, the word-by-word arrangement giving way to letter-by-letter treatment in their case. The justification is that prefixes are hardly separate words and have no significance out of their context. Fuller details and illustrations of this matter will be found in the chapters on Persons (IV g) and Places (III o).

(d) *Alphabetical Order: Persons*

Surnames are placed after all places of the same spelling, whether or not the latter are qualified, as is shown in the recent Stoke example. Their treatment differs from that of place names in that they are not repeated for each individual, second and subsequent persons of the same name being merely indented from the surname. Surnames therefore present fewer problems of arrangement than do place names. Other than those mentioned in the last paragraph we need only note that hyphenated names and those containing apostrophes are treated as single words, the hyphens and apostrophes being ignored; that homonymous surnames of different nationalities should be repeated for each nationality; that names containing accented letters should follow identical names without them, although accents otherwise should not affect alphabetical order; and that names beginning 'M"', 'Mc' and 'Mac' should be arranged in the index and among themselves as if they all began 'Mac'. (For examples see IV i.) As in the case of place names, the obsolete or variant forms of surnames should be arranged in strict alphabetical order after the modern or chosen spelling in the main index entry, and alphabetically adjacent obsolete or variant forms grouped together into a composite cross-reference must also be in alphabetical order (see IV b).

We have already seen that there are certain persons who are invariably indexed by their forenames. These forenames must be repeated for each different person. When there are people with a surname which is identical to a forename they follow all those who are indexed by that forename, and the latter are arranged among themselves in the order: biblical saints, other saints, popes, emperors, kings of England, kings of other countries in alphabetical order of their countries, other members of sovereign houses in the same order, friars, and others known by their forenames. When there are two or more popes or monarchs of the same country with the same forename, they should follow each other in numerical order. (For examples see IV j.) All this is not really in breach of alphabetical order. At any point where there is congestion resulting from homonymous headings alphabetical order can be usefully supplemented by an intelligent and consistent application of a hierarchical, numerical or other easily appreciated arrangement.

The subheadings of surnames consist basically of forenames, which can be given in strict alphabetical order under the word-by-word rules. Persons whose forenames are not known come first; persons who are known only by the initials of their forenames precede those whose first forenames begin with the same letter as the first initial; and persons with one forename precede those with the same forename and an initial, who are in turn followed by those with the same first forename and another or others. (For examples see IV k.) The various ways in which indexers should distinguish persons with identical surname and forenames are described in detail in the chapter on Persons (IV n). Here it is sufficient to say that it is usually the alphabetical order of whatever extra pieces of information are included concerning them for this purpose which determines their order in relation to each other. Only occasionally does such an alphabetical arrangement have to be supplemented. One such case is when peers share the same names and title, when their dates are the determining element (IV m). But when commoners have identical names and the only extra information known about them, or the only extra information which distinguishes them, is their titles, ranks or styles—Dr, Lord, Mrs, Sir, Major, etc.—such persons should be arranged in the alphabetical, not hierarchical, order of their titles, any without such titles preceding those with them. In all other cases, although such titles should always appear in the index before the forenames, they should be disregarded for purposes of alphabetising (IV k). Finally, it is occasionally difficult to decide exactly what the correct alphabetical order of identically named persons is when each is described in a different way for purposes of differentiation, and one arrangement can be of equal merit with another, as illustrated in section IV n.

Any modifications of an individual's entry or subentry should normally be alphabetically arranged. This applies to those based on the offices which he held. There is sometimes a temptation to give them in chronological or hierarchical order, but they can be more easily arranged alphabetically, and alphabetical order should never be breached anywhere in an index unless there are over-riding reasons for doing so. A legitimate and desirable exception to this rule, however, can be made for those persons some of whose modifications relate to their official positions and the others to their relatives, usually daughters, sons and wives, who are normally but not invariably known by their forenames. In such cases a single alphabetical sequence is less helpful than two, and it has been recommended that the offices should come first in alphabetical order, followed by relatives in the alphabetical order of their forenames or, if their names are not known, of their relationships (IV m).

(e) *Alphabetical Order: Subjects*
When the use of homonymous subject headings cannot be avoided they should be defined in round brackets and arranged alphabetically among themselves by the words of definition. The title of any organization, book or journal which is identical to a subject heading should follow it in the index. Homonymous subject headings must be repeated for each of their meanings. (For examples see V d.)

The modifications of subject entries are often more complex than those of persons and places, but they should still be arranged, wherever possible, in strict alphabetical order. That order must be determined by the first word of each modification, whether or not it is the most significant word. But there are four types of subject entry (illustrated in V g) for which a single alphabetical sequence can justifiably be dispensed with. One is when there are modifications relating to the main heading, and also specific subheadings. They are much more useful and clearer if arranged in separate alphabets in that order. Two others are those which contain items (subheadings or modifications) which can be usefully grouped and those which contain named items. These items should not be dispersed among the other subentries, but should be arranged in their own alphabetical sequence or sequences at the end. The subheadings of these items should usually themselves be in alphabetical order, although there is a case for having named items at the very end even in breach of that order. Finally, when there are a number of modifications which are identical except for varying numbers or values mentioned in them, it is far better to arrange them among themselves in numerical rather than in alphabetical order, although they must jointly be in their correct alphabetical position among the other modifications.

(f) *Alphabetical Order: General Indexes*
In General Indexes subject headings which are identical in spelling to place names (or their significant words) and/or surnames come after both of them,

followed by any titles. The only major breach with alphabetical order which is to be found almost exclusively in General Indexes is in the arrangement of the subject modifications of the most important persons and places. Their modifications can often be more usefully set out in chronological order, although there will sometimes be a few which are of too general a nature to be chronologically arranged and which can be given in alphabetical order before the chronological sequence begins. If such hybrid entries are numerous and the general modifications form a sizable proportion of the whole, it is probably better to revert to a single alphabetical arrangement (see VI a).

This chapter has inevitably been largely filled with exceptions. It is therefore best to end it by re-emphasising the rules. Indexes should be set out with their entries arranged in strict alphabetical order, and there must be overriding reasons for departing from a single alphabetical sequence for their subentries. For indexes to record publications the word-by-word method of alphabetising should be used.

CHAPTER VIII

REFERENCES

(a) *Entry and Page Numbers*

The basic question whether the numbers in the index are to represent pages or entries has to be decided before the preparation of the text is started. In days when printing was relatively inexpensive index references were normally to pages, as they inevitably are in secondary works still. It did not matter that the text remained in page proof for months while the index was completed or even entirely compiled and that a further delay ensued, while the index went through its proof stages, before the volume could be printed off, bound and published. Today, high printing costs make it essential, wherever possible, for indexes to record publications, which are necessarily much longer than those to secondary works, to be compiled before any part of the volume goes to press. This means indexing by entry numbers. Most records break down readily into fairly short entries, which can be numbered consecutively throughout the volume. Two or three entries to the page is the ideal: this greatly facilitates the finding of a particular person or place if there are many on the page. The entries must, of course, be natural divisions of the original records: single inquisitions, individual entries on Chancery rolls, individual cases on plea rolls, and so on. It does not matter how short they are, but if it is impossible to restrict an entry to less than two pages, one of two courses has to be followed. One is to insert the relevant page number in brackets after the entry number on every occurrence of the reference in the index, thus

Alexander, William, 299 (p 82)

But such mixed references are clumsy and, of course, they cannot be completed until the text is in page proof, for which reason it is better to adopt the second course if such lengthy entries are numerous. This involves the breaking up of such entries into a number of subdivisions, the breaks being natural ones wherever possible, otherwise being superimposed at regular intervals. The subdivisions should be marked (a), (b), (c), etc., or (i), (ii), (iii). The above example might then read

Alexander, William, 299 (iv)

This is also clumsy, but at least it can be completed while the text is in manuscript or typescript and the subdivisions of entries can be kept fairly short.

Index references to the Introduction to the volume are normally to pages, and in order that they may be readily distinguished from references to the text without the use of 'p' and 'pp' it is advisable for the Introduction to be paginated in small roman numerals, running on consecutively from the page numbers of the preliminary matter. They contrast markedly in the index with the arabic entry numbers, as this example shows

Bright, John, iii, vii, 19, 40, 116

This use of small roman numerals makes it desirable to use large romans for volume numbers in indexes which cover two or more volumes.

(b) *Volume Numbers*

Single indexes which cover two or more volumes are extremely useful, especially when the printing of a large record, such as a bishop's register, requires a number of volumes of the Canterbury and York Society or of a local record society's publications. It is much more useful to have all the references to a particular place or person gathered together under a single index entry than to have them split up in perhaps as many as six volumes. Similarly, it is invaluable to have just one compendious index to a series of publications for a whole reign, such as that to the four volumes of the *Calendar of Close Rolls* for Henry IV's reign and that to the five volumes of the *Calendar of Patent Rolls* for Edward VI's. The disadvantage is that there is often a very long interval between the publication of the first volume and the appearance of the index (eleven years in the case of the Henry IV Close Rolls), during which the usefulness of the volumes is considerably less than if they had individual indexes. In the ideal world, of course, every volume would have its own index and there would also be a composite index to all the volumes in the series. But those who have read this book to this point will appreciate that indexes are compiled in a far from perfect world.

Those single indexes to runs of volumes which have so far been produced have given their references in a number of different ways. Sometimes, as with *The Book of Fees*, the various volumes which share an index have a single pagination, or numeration of entries, running consecutively from the beginning of the first to the end of the last. The index references are therefore merely to page or entry numbers, which is the sole purpose of the consecutive numeration. This has the virtue of simplicity, and is the best system to adopt provided that the first and last pages or entry numbers are clearly stamped on the spine of each volume so that the user is not left to guess to which volume he must turn. But when each volume of text begins with page or entry number one, a more complex reference is required. Some indexes, such as that to the Edward VI *Calendar of Patent Rolls*, use small roman numerals for volume numbers, as follows

Brown, Thomas, i. 36; iii. 155, 502;

v. 89

As suggested in the last section, this usage is liable to cause confusion with references to the Introduction, especially when the references are all in one volume. Thus

Brown, Thomas, v. 89

meaning page or entry 89 in volume V, is only slightly different from

Brown, Thomas, v, 89

which refers to page v of the Introduction and to page or entry 89 of the text. Another frequently encountered usage is for the volume numbers to be in arabics in bold type, thus

Brown, Thomas, **1** 36; **3** 155, 502; **5** 89

which is clear. Unfortunately its use makes it impossible for bold type to be used to emphasise particular references, for which it is often required (see VIII d; XI g). There is too little difference between

Brown, Thomas, **5** 89

meaning, again, page or entry 89 in volume V, and

Brown, Thomas, **5**, 89

which normally indicates that there is an important mention of Thomas Brown on page or in entry 5 and a less important one at 89. It is therefore best to use large roman numerals for volume numbers, so that our original example would read

Brown, Thomas, I 36; III 155, 502;

V 89

There is no need for any form of punctuation after the volume numbers—the index to the Henry IV *Calendar of Close Rolls* uses large romans followed by commas. We shall shortly see that one of the cardinal rules of indexing is to use no more punctuation than is essential for the avoidance of ambiguity and confusion (X a–c).

(c) *Footnotes*

Footnotes can be referred to in the index in one of two ways. One is by using an asterisk,

Johnson, Hugh, 59*

indicating that Hugh Johnson occurs in a footnote to page or entry 59. This usage has two minor disadvantages: the reference is imprecise if the page or entry has more than one footnote, and the asterisk might be interpreted as emphasising the importance of the reference to 59. A prefatory note explaining the significance of asterisks would be essential. The second method of indicating footnotes—by the use of 'n' and 'nn'—is preferable. The previous index entry could thereby be rendered

Johnson, Hugh, 59 (n 2)

or, if necessary,

Johnson, Hugh, 59 (nn 2–4)

This is both more exact and also self-explanatory. When the footnotes are not numbered, but are represented by a series of signs

Johnson, Hugh, 59n

is no less precise and is more immediately intelligible than

Johnson, Hugh, 59*

although footnotes ought always to be numbered for ease of reference.

(d) *Important References*

When there are several references to a person, place or subject and one is far more important than the others, it is often useful to emphasise the important one. In indexes to record publications such emphasis should not depend upon the subjective judgment of the indexer as to what is important. His judgment would inevitably be different from that of many of the users, and it would anyway be almost impossible to apply it consistently throughout the index while dealing with all the other problems of indexing. The emphasis must rather have an exact significance, which is constant throughout, immediately apparent from the text and therefore easily applicable to the index, as in the indexes to the *Calendar of Inquisitions Post Mortem* where all references to inquisitions held on the death of a tenant-in-chief are distinguished under his name from all the more casual references to him by typographical emphasis.

Index references can be emphasised in various ways. One is by printing any significant ones first, the more casual references following in their normal numerical order. Thus in the following example

Marsh, Henry atte, 216, 34, 89, 176,
254, 320

216 is printed out of sequence to emphasise it. But there are drawbacks to this practice. A user who is interested only in the very early entries in the volume and who sees that the first reference is to entry 216, which he knows is beyond his chronological limits, may assume that the subsequent references consist of higher numbers and so may miss relevant material. More important, if entry 34 in the last example had been the important one, some other type of emphasis

would have had to be used, as it would if there was only one reference to a person and it was a significant one. It is unthinkable that such references should remain unemphasised while comparable ones in other entries are stressed, but to use two different conventions in a single index to convey exactly the same meaning is too complicated and clumsy. It is therefore far better to emphasise all important references typographically, as is done by the use of bold type in the last-mentioned *Calendar*. The previous example can thereby be rendered either

> Marsh, Henry atte, **216**, 34, 89, 176,
> 254, 320

or

> Marsh, Henry atte, 34, 89, 176, **216**,
> 254, 320

The former combines the two main methods of emphasis, but is rather excessive and does not completely obviate the first of the drawbacks inherent in merely putting the important entry first. It is as well not to distinguish important references by marking them with asterisks because of the possibility that they will be thought to indicate footnotes, with the implication that such references are not the most but the least important.

(e) *Consecutive References*

When a person, place or subject occurs in a number of consecutive entries or on a number of consecutive pages, the first and last entries or pages should always be specified in the index thus

> London, 54-82

Usages to be avoided are

> London, 54 ff.
> London, 54 foll.
> London, 54 *et seqq.*

These are much less helpful for the user, while the provision of the exact range of pages is no greater trouble for the indexer. The least number of figures should normally be used to represent such a run of references as long as no ambiguity results. The left hand column below shows correct usages, the second and third columns incorrect ones

26-8	26-28	
126-8	126-28	126-128
124-42	124-142	
2224-8	2224-28	2224-228
2305-8	2305-08	2305-308

Some authorities recommend that the last two figures of the second number should always be printed unless the penultimate one is a nought. They would use 26-28, 126-28 and 2224-28 in the last examples. This doctrine possibly arose because of the practice of some indexers of previous generations to use, for example, 331—2 to indicate page 331 of volume II. But volume numbers are never so printed today and it is difficult to see any advantage in the inclusion of the penultimate figure. The exception, on which all authorities agree, is that figures from 10 to 19 should be set out in full, whether they stand alone or follow hundreds or thousands. Again the left hand column is correct, the right incorrect

15-17	15-7
315-17	315-7
2015-17	2015-7

It is difficult to justify this practice by any argument other than that numbers from 10 to 19, unlike most subsequent ones, tend not to be thought of as composite numbers and that they are represented by a single word. But the practice is consistently used and must be justified by this consistency, which presumably results from its looking right. It is adopted automatically by most indexers, and the small saving of space which would result from omitting the penultimate figure would be negligible compared with the upsetting of an ingrained habit. In indexing, many small points require thought; their number should not be increased without a strong reason.

There are two other kinds of terminal numbers which must also be written in full. One is when the run begins with a two-figure number and ends with a three-figure one, or continues from one hundred into the next or from the nine-hundreds to beyond a thousand. One should then follow the usages illustrated in the left-hand column, never any of the others

95-103	95-3	95-03
365-413	365-13	
992-1001	992-1	992-01	992-001

Secondly, it is better not to abbreviate roman numerals at all because of their greater inherent complexity. For example, xliv-xlix is much clearer than xliv-ix. Very little extra space will be consumed if small romans are confined to pages of the Introduction (see VIII a).

When references are to pages it is useful to distinguish between casual mentions of a person, place or subject on consecutive pages and continuous treatment of it there.

Edward, prince of Wales, 69-71

indicates that the prince is the subject, or one of the subjects, of a passage which begins on page 69 and continues throughout page 70 and onto page 71. By contrast

Edward, prince of Wales, 69, 70, 71

means that although he appears on all three pages the occurrences are intermittent or unconnected. When references are to entries, however, it is unnecessary to make this distinction. It will be assumed that the entries are separate entities and that a run of numbers will therefore probably not indicate continuous treatment of the same matter. First and last references are therefore adequate for either type of run in volumes indexed by entry numbers. Similarly it should never be necessary to state in the index how many times a person, place or subject occurs in a single entry. However casual some of the mentions, they will be more easily findable in the normally shorter entries than on the longer and often crowded pages. It can be assumed that there may be more than one occurrence of the matter in the entry, even if it is not a vital part of it, and that the searcher, however short his time, will read the whole entry for the sake of the context and will thus miss nothing relevant. But when references are to pages and a person, place or subject occurs several times on a single page, but haphazardly or in different contexts, it is useful to indicate this in the index so that the searcher does not miss anything relevant to his interests. Sometimes the number of separate occurrences on a page are given as follows

Edward, prince of Wales, 27 (3), 62 (2)

This means that Edward is mentioned three times on page 27 and twice on page 62, but in different passages or connections. Several occurrences of his name in the same passage would not be noted, since the user must be credited with a desire to read the whole of the relevant section of the page. This use of numbers, however, is liable to suggest, especially to a searcher turning to the volume after using one in which subdivisions of entries are similarly indicated (see VIII a), that they are subdivisions of pages. It is therefore preferable to use Latin terms. Sometimes they are written

Edward, prince of Wales, 27 ter, 62 bis

but, because it is useful to have all such details in brackets (see X g), the following is recommended in preference

Edward, prince of Wales, 27 (ter), 62
(bis)

If there are more than three distinct mentions of the same name on a page, although there should rarely be, the index reference should take the form

Edward, prince of Wales, 189 passim

The use of the first and last pages or entry numbers of a run, discussed earlier in this section, should mean that the person, place or subject occurs at least once on every page or in every entry from the first to the last mentioned. But if it occurs frequently over a long run of pages or entries, but on not quite every one, the first and last pages should be followed by the word passim. Thus

Edward, prince of Wales, 2, 3, 7-16, 22,
54-97 passim, 102-4, 111-19,
130, 152-78 passim, 212

shows that the prince appears on every page or in every entry from 7 to 16, 102 to 104 and 111 to 119, all inclusive, as well as in the individual ones cited, but in not quite every one in the two series 54-97 and 152-78. It should be mentioned that in this section the use of long runs of numbers and of the word passim has been dealt with from the purely technical point of view. The desirability of having such references and the alternatives, such as breaking them down by the use of modifications, will be discussed later (VIII f). Here it must suffice to add that the single reference passim is not to be encouraged. For example

Westminster, Midd, writs dated at,
passim

means that the great majority of entries contain a writ dated at Westminster. It is better to state in the Introduction that, unless otherwise shown in the text, all writs are dated at Westminster. The Westminster place-date need then never appear in the text—a considerable saving of space—and the index item would refer to the Introduction thus

Westminster, Midd, writs dated at, iv

(For further illustrations of this use of the Introduction see V a.)

(f) *Numerous References*

Whenever possible, long strings of numerical references should be avoided. This is usually easily achieved with subject entries, which can be broken down by the use of modifications. Thus instead of

Chancery, 7, 11, 29, 54, 96, 110-20,
131, 154, 198-9, 217, 225, 233,
249, 288, 332, 360-6 the entry should be subdivided in some such way as

> Chancery, 11, 96, 131, 233, 332
> > bail given in, 110-20
> > dower assigned in, 360-6
> > examinations in, 29, 288
> > pleas in, 7, 54, 131, 217
> > records shown in, 154, 198-9
> > rolls of, 225, 249

Some indexers prefer not to have numbers immediately following the main heading so that it can stand on a line of its own. It is then necessary to arrange the casual references at the end, and the above entry would run

> Chancery
> > bail given in, 110-20
> > dower assigned in, 360-6
> > examinations in, 29, 288
> > pleas in, 7, 54, 131, 217
> > records shown in, 154, 198-9
> > rolls of, 225, 249
> > other mentions, 11, 96, 131, 233, 332

The word 'references' is sometimes found instead of 'other mentions'. The desirability or otherwise of having headings on a line of their own will be considered later (XI f). Here we may merely note that the slight advantage of having the least important references at the end of the entry is counterbalanced by their often being out of alphabetical order.

Persons and places are sometimes more difficult to break down. As we have already seen (V a; VIII e), when a subject modification of a person or place would result in references to the majority of entries in the volume a single reference to the Introduction is the solution. But most modifications of persons and places, and indeed of subjects, are included in the index less to break down large lists of numbers than because of their inherent value. We have already seen that certain modifications should be used whenever relevant irrespective of whether the numerical references are many or few. Thus 'writs dated at' should always appear in order to separate such routine mentions of places from those which are more likely to interest local historians (see III j); and references to a person in his private capacity should be distinguished from those concerning him as an office holder (IV m). Such modifications may themselves have a fairly large number of references, and while it is obviously undesirable to have a solid block of references, perhaps running to a dozen lines, it is as bad to introduce unnecessary and useless modifications, or modifications of modifications, just for the sake of breaking them down. All modifications should be natural ones in that each should relate to an aspect of a person, place or subject with which some searchers might be exclusively concerned. Moreover, users will justifiably assume that the types of modifications found in one entry will be used in similar entries throughout the index; and that when entries, however few their references, are not so modified, it is because they are incapable of such modification. It therefore follows that it will not always be possible to limit the number of undifferentiated references to a person, place or subject, or the number of references to each modification, to three or four, as is often recommended. That may be an admirable rule for short indexes to secondary works, but it should not be rigidly applied to the longer indexes to record publications.

(g) *Prefatory Notes*

Prefatory notes to indexes have already been recommended at several points in this work: to show the main headings under which grouped subjects are indexed (V b), to explain any breaches with alphabetical order in General Indexes (VI a), to indicate the existence of any special index (VI b), and to define any abbreviations used other than those of counties (IV k, m). But such notes are particularly desirable to explain any unusual features connected with the references. Because the references in indexes to secondary works are almost invariably to pages, it is advisable to state in the prefatory note when references are to entries. A brief explanation of any use of roman numerals for pages of the Introduction or volume numbers, and of any conventions to indicate footnotes and important references should also be given.

But it should never be necessary to append such warning notes at the foot of every page of the index, as is advocated by some authorities. That would be disproportionate to the size of any conceivable difficulty. Conventional signs and abbreviations should always be simple and their significance clear. The reader would naturally turn to the beginning of the index for any necessary explanations of them. As to the references themselves, since it is recommended that there should normally be two or three entries to the page, the range of the reference numbers, often running into four figures, should make it immediately obvious that they are entry and not page numbers. If not, a single failure to find a person, place or subject on the page will alert the user to the fact that he should seek the corresponding entry, especially if the entry numbers in the text are in bold type, as they should be, to attract immediate attention. Also, of course, as more and more volumes are indexed in this way, searchers will increasingly expect indexes to refer to entries.

CHAPTER IX
CROSS-REFERENCES

(a) *General*

In earlier chapters we considered practices which result in a very considerable reduction in the number of cross-references in the index, although that is not always their sole purpose. Omitting the name of the county from cross-references makes it possible to use one cross-reference to serve a number of homonymous places and sometimes a surname as well, and the number can be increased if adjectival parts of place names are also omitted from cross-references, as is advised (III c); giving the modern forms of places in the text of calendars and descriptive lists obviates the need for the numerous cross-references from the manuscript forms to the modern ones (see III d); using standard forms of surnames in the index avoids the necessity for most cross-references from variant forms in volumes of post-medieval records (IV b); and noting at the beginning of the Subject Index the main headings under which subjects are grouped makes it unnecessary to cross-refer from synonyms and specific subjects to those headings (V b), although such cross-references are always desirable in General Indexes (VI a). At various points direct references to the text have been recommended as being more useful than cross-references (III k; IV l, m; V e); and, indeed, whatever their merits, cross-references are by their nature inferior to direct references. The invariable rule should be: when in doubt, refer directly to the text.

This chapter, however, is not concerned with the merits and demerits of cross-references, but merely with the techniques of cross-referring. However greatly the need for them is reduced, some cross-references will always be essential: from parishes to places within them (see III e), between surnames which may or may not be the same, between subjects which have overlapping interests (V b), and so on; and records printed in full transcript will always require indexes with a large number of cross-references (III c; IV b). All this is dealt with in the earlier chapters. Here we shall consider in turn the various kinds of cross-references as distinguished by the words which introduce them.

(b) *See*

In indexes to record publications the simple cross-reference '*see*' is most frequently used. It is used to direct the user from obsolete forms of place names to the modern spellings under which the references appear (III c), to the forms of surnames under which people are indexed from the variant spellings (IV b), from peerages and bishoprics to the family names of their holders (IV m), from pseudonyms to real names or *vice versa*, and possibly from one name to another in the case of persons who had alternative surnames or who changed their names (IV c, d). Similar cross-references have been recommended from the great offices of state in the Subject Index to the specific officials in the Index of Persons and Places (V e), while within the Subject Index itself, or the subject element of a General Index, it is often necessary to cross-refer from one or more synonyms to another under which the references appear, from one antonym, usually the negative one, to another (positive) one, from part of a compound subject heading to the complete heading, and from one or more significant words in a heading to the form of the heading under which the references are given (V b, c). We may take an example from the last-mentioned type as a reminder of the form which it is recommended that '*see*' cross-references should take. If there is an index entry headed 'London Corresponding Society' there should be a cross-reference

Corresponding Society see London
Corresponding Society

and possibly a similar cross-reference from 'Societies' to that and other specific societies.

These uses of '*see*' cross-references are fairly simple and straightforward, but a few warnings may not be out of place. One must never cross-refer to another cross-reference.

Documents see Records
Records see Manuscripts

is intolerable. Far worse is the completion of the circle with

Manuscripts see Documents

the searcher being left angry and without references after his efforts. Such atrocities are rarely perpetrated. One more frequently finds that references to the same subject are dispersed among two or more synonyms. The alternatives here are either to bring all the references together under the most likely heading and to cross-refer to it from all reasonable synonyms or, if there are no modifications or subheadings and the references are few so that it would take up no more space, to give them all, and it must be all, under every reasonable synonym. The latter course is obviously helpful, and references are far better than cross-references, other things being equal. The word 'reasonable' should be emphasised. The indexer should cross-refer from or index under any heading which an intelligent searcher could be expected to look up, given the nature of the particular volume, but should not go out of his way to discover every possible alternative word. The numerical references must never be given under more than one spelling of any surname, however many people share it, and place-name references always follow the modern form.

Cross-references are not required between entries which would be adjacent, since it can be assumed that anybody looking for, say, an obsolete or variant form of a name which would have been cross-referred from will immediately see instead the chosen form. But in all other cases they are required, however close they may be to the entries to which they cross-refer. It cannot be assumed that the searcher will necessarily find an entry which is only a few places away from where he expected to find it. When, however, there are adjacent entries all of which cross-refer to the same chosen heading, or to homonymous headings even if one is a place name, or the significant word thereof, and another a surname, it is wasteful of space to give them individually as

Berwyck see Berwick
Berwycke see Berwick
Berwyk see Berwick

They should rather be combined into a single entry reading

Berwyck, Berwycke, Berwyk see Berwick

Similarly, if two places whose modern spellings differ share an obsolete form, a single composite cross-reference is to be recommended, for example

Haghton see Haughton; Hawton

More examples and consideration of different aspects of such cross-references will be found in other chapters (III c; X d).

So far we have dealt with cross-references from one main heading to another: an alternative heading which is preferred. Simple '*see*' cross-references can also be used from one subentry to another under the same heading. We have already seen (IV l) that it is sometimes desirable to index a husband and wife, or a father and son, separately and to arrange them among all the other people with the same surname in the alphabetical order of their forenames. In order that the relationship should not be hidden from the searcher it is helpful in such cases to cross-refer between them as follows

Hilton, Anne, 72, 96
      husband of *see* William
Henry, 36
John, 54, 122
Richard, 314
Robert, 27, 59
William, 72, 154
      wife of *see* Anne

The longer and more complex the entry, the more useful such internal cross-references are. When they are used within a large subject entry it is useful to use the words '*see* A *below*' and '*see* B *above*'. Alternatively, and equally good when it is feasible, the entry can be recast and '*q.v.*' used, as follows

Hilton, Anne wife of William (*q.v.*), 72,
96

with an equivalent description and direction under William.

(c) *See under*

The direction '*see*' usually refers the user to another item in the index in a similar hierarchical position: from one main heading to another or from one subheading to another. '*See under*' directs him from a specific subject (it is nearly always a subject) to the main heading under which it has been grouped. Thus if there is a heading 'Occupations', with all the particular occupations grouped under it, the cross-references from each of them in its alphabetical position in the index should take the form

Carpenter *see under* Occupations

It would not be positively misleading to use

Carpenter *see* Occupations

but it is slightly less exact, and the saving of one word does not compensate for the loss of the useful distinction between '*see*' and '*see under*'. '*See under* A *below*' and '*see under* B *above*' are occasionally of use within very complex entries, 'A' and 'B' being subheadings and, of course, in the lower case. Thus in a General Index one might under 'Spain' have in the appropriate alphabetical position the internal cross-reference

ships *see under* navy *above*

This warns the searcher to look in the same entry and not under 'N' in the index as a whole.

(d) *See also*

Both '*see*' and '*see under*' direct the searcher to the place where all the references to a person, place or subject are to be found. Cross-references introduced by the words '*see also*' direct him from an entry or subentry which has references of its own to one or more entries or subentries where there are further references. '*See also under*' is similarly used to cross-refer from an entry or subentry to one or more subentries. Before discussing the circumstances in which these cross-references are used, we must consider where they should be placed. When they cross-refer from main headings they can be put either at the beginning of the entries or at the end. If they are at the beginning there are four possible ways of printing them. The first

> Household articles. *See also* Furniture

has the disadvantage that it makes it difficult to have numerical references depending on the heading alone. If they are inserted between 'articles' and '*See also*' the point of having the cross-reference at the beginning is weakened. It is separated from the heading and also appears to relate to the unmodified references alone and not to the whole entry with its modifications. The unmodified references could be relegated to the end of the entry and introduced by the words 'other mentions' (see VIII f), but consistency would then demand that this should be done throughout the index which might not be feasible because of the extra space consumed when all headings stand on lines of their own. In the second usage, namely

> Household articles (*see also* Furniture)

numerical references can follow the final bracket, but the appearance is rather clumsy. The other two are for indexes in which headings normally stand on lines of their own. For greater clarity the cross-references should either be indented beyond the normal indentation of modifications, as follows

> Household articles
>> *See also* Furniture
>
> carried off by outlaws, 29
> destroyed by floods, 67
> Household articles
>> (*See also* Furniture)
>
> carried off by outlaws, 29
> destroyed by floods, 67

or not indented at all, thus

> Household articles
> *See also* Furniture
>> carried off by outlaws, 29
>> destroyed by floods, 67
>
> Household articles
> (*See also* Furniture)
>> carried off by outlaws, 29
>> destroyed by floods, 67

The versions with the brackets are the better ones in that with multiple cross-references which happen to complete a line there can be no temporary confusion with the first modification. But the main argument against all the usages so far illustrated is that the cross-references are given priority over the entry itself and its own references and subentries. It is reasonable to assume that anyone who looks up an entry is primarily interested in the references given under that head, that he will work through them and those of the subentries and only when he has exhausted them, if then, will he want to turn to cognate entries. The logical position for '*see also*' cross-references is therefore at the very end, and it is recommended that they be indented to the same extent as the first modification or subheading, as in the following example

Household articles, 54, 163, 339
   carried off by outlaws, 29
   destroyed by floods, 67
   types of
      basins, 144, 250
      bellows, 448
      carpets, 166
      dishes, 40, 70
      jars, 54
      knives, 72
      pans, 212, 250, 352
      plates, 40, 114
      pots, 54, 114
      spoons, 72, 143
      towels, 53, 166
   See also Furniture

The objection to this usage is that it can lead to uncertainty as to whether the cross-references relate to the whole entry or to the final subentry. In practice there is rarely serious confusion even in cases when neither the sense nor the lay out is as helpful as in the last example. Cross-references from modifications should be very few indeed (and to them even fewer), and even from subheadings they should be infrequent. When they are necessary they should run on directly from the last numerical reference in this way

Household articles, 54, 163, 339
   types of
      basins, 144, 250
      knives, 72. *See also under* Weapons
      spoons, 72, 143
   See also Furniture

If this is done consistently throughout the index, the indexer need have no qualms about having misled his users.

Most '*see also*' cross-references are reciprocal. That is because they link distinct but allied subjects: subjects of equal importance which have overlapping interests but which cannot be conveniently grouped together. Each must therefore cross-refer to the other. Thus if there is a '*see also*' cross-reference from 'Customs and Excise' to 'Taxation', there should also be one from 'Taxation' to 'Customs and Excise'. It may occasionally happen that the numerical references under both are identical, in which case they should be deleted from one and the '*see also*' cross-reference should be replaced by a modified form of the simple cross-reference, namely

Customs and Excise *see* Taxation *all*
references

Normally, however, even if some of the references are common others are different, or additional in respect of one of the entries, so that reciprocal cross-references are appropriate. They are absolutely essential when one entry has modifications which could just as well have been given under the other, as might happen with 'Marriage' and 'Divorce', although, as we have already seen

(V c), such subjects should be brought together unless that would produce too unwieldy an entry.

Some 'see also' cross-references are one way only. They usually refer from a general heading to one or more associated specific subjects which themselves form entries of such a length or complexity as to make it undesirable for them to be grouped as subentries under the general heading. Thus the general subject 'Agriculture' might, for many kinds of records, require the cross-reference

See also Crops; Farm equipment;
Livestock

without there necessarily being any need of a similar cross-reference from the specific subjects back to 'Agriculture', although this may sometimes be given from at least some of them. Such multiple cross-references from the general to the specific can occasionally be numerous. In a few indexes the entries cross-referred to have even been classified into three or four types of subjects in the cross-reference, each separately alphabetised and arranged in a paragraph of its own. This is to be discouraged. It is better to abolish the cross-reference altogether and rely on an index note or the Introduction to perform the same service. But it is usually possible to avoid a long string of cross-references by a form of words such as

Officials, 6, 54, 139, 512
imprisonment of, 99
oaths of office of, 334
See also titles of individual officials

But too much must not be made of lengthy and complex cross-references. Whereas the indexer has scope for innumerable simple cross-references from synonyms, although he must restrain his ingenuity, reciprocal and multiple cross-references are inevitably limited by the nature of the index and the number and arrangement of the entries.

Sometimes it is convenient to retain one or two specific subjects in their correct alphabetical positions in the index because of the length or complexity of the entries, while grouping all the others of the same genus under a general heading. Those excluded can either be cross-referred to from the general entry in the usual way by the use of 'see also', or thus

Illnesses and Diseases, 22, 25, 107
cured, 32
procured by witchcraft, 216
types of
ague, 249, 268
blood poisoning, 9
epilepsy, 228, 325
gangrene, 25
plague see that heading
syphilis, 144

Alternatively, and rather better, the penultimate line could read

plague, q.v.

But neither 'q.v.' nor 'see that heading' would be appropriate for the cross-reference to 'Furniture' in our recent 'Household articles' example, because 'Furniture' is a much more general subject than the individual items which form the subentries there, so that it could not have been alphabetised with them.

The desirability of 'see also' cross-references between places and persons, and between subjects and either persons or places has already been discussed (IV m; V e) and it was recommended that they be kept to a minimum, being used mainly to cross-refer from peerages, bishoprics and the great offices of state to the names of their holders. Here we are concerned with the purely technical aspect, and the important thing in an entry beginning

> Chancellors, 16, 72, 98, 156, 332. *See*
>   *also* Index of Persons and Places
>   *under* Morton, John; Warham,
>   William; Wolsey, Thomas

is that the straight numerical references must be either to mentions of chancellors unknown or to the chancellor whoever he may be. What is indefensible is that the searcher should be told to turn to Morton, Warham and Wolsey only for him to find that he is confronted with the previous numerical references, although it will, of course, occasionally happen that the same entry or page in the text mentions both a named and an unnamed official. When there are no numerical references after the unmodified heading in entries such as the last, '*see*' replaces '*see also*', but whichever is used this type of cross-reference must precede any modifications. This does not conflict with the rule given above, that cross-references to cognate subjects should come at the end of subject entries, because the cross-references to officials holding the office or title which forms the heading are either substitutes for numerical references or additions to them. Hence they should be preceded only by any numerical references of the unmodified heading. Indeed, it is useful to have the differences between the two uses of these cross-references underlined by placing them at the beginning or the end of entries according to their significance. The difference can be further pointed by using '*and see*' in lieu of '*see also*' at the beginning of entries, so that our last example could equally well read

> Chancellors, 16, 72, 98, 156, 332, *and*
>   *see* Index of Persons and Places
>   *under* Morton, John; Warham,
>   William; Wolsey, Thomas

The use of a comma instead of a full stop after the last reference allows the cross-reference to run on more naturally. But '*and see*' is ungainly if used on a line of its own at the end of an entry, while the word '*and*' tends to link the cross-reference to the line immediately above it. '*See also*' must therefore be used there.

(e) *q.v.*

In the recent example headed 'Illnesses and Diseases' it would, as we have seen (IX d), have been permissible and even preferable to have used '*q.v.*', standing for '*quod vide*', instead of '*see that heading*' or, with a different wording or arrangement, '*see*' or '*see also*'. There are two other kinds of cross-reference for which '*q.v.*' is greatly to be preferred. They are from places to persons described in terms of them, for example

> Hastings, Sussex, Brown, Parks and
>   Sleigh of, *q.v.*

and from parishes to any places within them which are separately indexed, for example

> Saltash, Corn, Forder, Shillingham,
>   Tideford Quay and Trehan in,
>   *q.v.*

Further examples and a fuller consideration of this usage, with an explanation of
the advantages of '*q.v.*' over every other type of cross-reference in such cases,
will be found in section III e (see also III i, j; IV n).

(f) *Cf.*

It is often difficult to know whether to use '*cf.*', meaning 'compare', or '*see also*'.
'*Cf.*' should indicate a looser relationship between the headings to and from
which it refers than does '*see also*', but the borderline between them is inevitably
indistinct. We have seen (IX d) that '*see also*' should be used to cross-refer from
a generic subject entry to one or more of its specific elements and between
subjects which are so closely allied as to have some common ground. '*Cf.*',
which should always be used reciprocally, should rather link subjects which are
cognate but which do not overlap, for example

Taverns, 67, 394
Cf. Breweries
Breweries, 5, 97, 306
Cf. Taverns

The cross-reference is useful in such cases, when there is a good chance that at
least some of the searchers who are interested in one of the subjects will like to
know of the occurrence of the other. It will sometimes happen that when there
is a one-way '*see also*' cross-reference from a general heading to several specific
ones, it is appropriate to have '*cf.*' cross-references between two or more of the
latter, although not necessarily from every one to all the others. Thus the
general entry 'Lands' might end

See also Chases; Closes; Forests; Gar-
dens; Parks; Warrens; Woods

There would probably be reciprocal '*see also*' cross-references between 'Forests'
and 'Woods' because of their tendency to overlap, whereas reciprocal '*cf.*' cross-
references would be more appropriate between 'Chases', 'Parks' and 'Warrens'.
But the most valuable use of '*cf.*' in indexes to record publications is for cross-
referring between surnames which at the date of the documents may or may not
be variant forms of the same name but which were later quite distinct so that it is
unsafe to amalgamate them (see IV b).

(g) *Paragraphed Entries*

It will be more convenient to consider cross-references to and from entries
arranged in paragraph form after we have dealt with the other aspects of that
arrangement (XI d). Here we may note that the peculiarities of punctuation
which such entries demand make it essential to keep all cross-references to a
minimum and to place those which it is necessary to include either at the beginning or at the very end of the entries. This is a fitting theme with which to end
this chapter. We began with the statement that cross-references are inferior to
references, but this may have since been submerged under the details of cross-
reference technique. The mention of paragraphed entries serves as a useful
reminder of it.

CHAPTER X

PUNCTUATION

(a) *General*

The two main rules for the punctuation of indexes are: punctuation should be kept to a minimum; and that which is used should always have significance and should therefore be used consistently throughout the index. These rules are interconnected, one of the principal reasons for avoiding all inessential punctuation being that it makes clearer the specific function of what is retained. The other reason is the extra cost and enhanced possibility of errors, since punctuation is difficult to proof-read. For these reasons it has already been advised (III a) that hyphens should not be used in place names, although they must, of course, be included in any double-barrelled modern surnames which normally contain them (IV h, i). For the same and other reasons it has also been recommended that no marks of suspension be used at the end of obsolete forms of places and surnames (III c), the apostrophe being reserved for its normal uses. Again, until recently dots or rules were frequently employed at the beginning of all modifications to indicate repetition of the main heading, and sometimes of subheadings and earlier modifications also. But, as will be fully explained and illustrated later (XI a-e), these practices have been almost entirely superseded by indentation or paragraphing, or a combination of the two. Not only is the result more pleasing to the eye, but it is also less expensive to set up in type and less prone to typographical errors. An earlier practice, still occasionally recommended, was for all references to be on the extreme right of the column, any sizable space between them and the last word being filled with dots. Thus an entry would be printed as follows

Martin, Elizabeth wife of William 322, 714
 John 558, 561
 Roger 337
  bailiff of Northampton 32, 834
   deputy of 572
 William 322
  wife of *see* Elizabeth

The column has been deliberately widened because this usage flourished in the days when entries straddled the whole width of the page. It had little to recommend it then, but now that printed indexes are invariably in double columns it has nothing at all and it has fallen into almost complete disuse, references normally running straight on from the headings, subheadings and modifications to which they relate and being separated from them only by a comma (see X c, e). Dots, usually three however long or short the passage they represent, are reserved for words or parts of words omitted from the original manuscript or illegible there.

(b) *Full stops*

Similarly, until recently full stops normally followed the last numerical reference of every heading, subheading and modification, but they are unnecessary there. They add nothing to one's understanding of the entries and all have to be checked in proof, if cursorily. Today they are nearly always omitted. It is also recommended here that full stops be omitted after the normally accepted abbreviations of counties and, if used, of forenames. The recommended abbreviations (III h; IV k) are all clearly recognizable as the relevant counties and names, especially in their contexts, so that full stops are superfluous; and as an index is not a work of literature it is immaterial that some of them are contractions, which should never end with full stops, and the rest are suspensions, which elsewhere do. As to the use of letters to represent constantly recurring words—'w' for 'wife' or 'witness', 's' for 'son', 'd' for 'daughter' and 'j' for 'juror' or 'justice', to give the most likely examples—they are obviously abbreviations and so again do not need full stops; and the same applies to the generally recognized abbreviations of personal styles, and to 'sen', 'jun', and so on. (For more on abbreviations see IV k, m; VII a.) Yet another use of full stops—between volume numbers and page or entry numbers—is sometimes encountered in indexes covering more than one volume, but it is also quite unnecessary if large roman numerals are used to signify volumes as has been recommended (VIII b).

Indeed, there are only two uses of full stops in indexes which can be justified as a usual practice, and one of them should be encountered very infrequently. It occurs when initials alone constitute an index entry. We have already seen (IV a) that when a person is known solely by his initials and cannot be identified, so that it is uncertain whether they are genuine initials or a code, they should be indexed both straightforwardly and inverted to bring the last to the beginning, as follows

R.S.T., 67

T., R.S., 67

and also (V c) that organizations which occur in the text in the form of initials should normally have a cross-reference from the initials to the full title, such as

I.R.A. *see* Irish Republican Army

Some indexers omit the full stops in cases such as these, but it is clearer to have them, especially in indexes in which small capitals are used for headings of main entries, or the more important of them. In the interests of consistency full stops must also be used for the corresponding abbreviations in the main entries, as in

Irish Republican Army (I.R.A.), 332

or, if a person is known in the text sometimes by initials only and sometimes by his full name,

Brown, Matthew, (M.B.), 56, 72, 594

By contrast, when a person's surname is always used but his forenames are represented by initials, the initials do not require full stops because their significance will be clear, as in

Dodwell, Mrs J M, 66

There is also one exceptional type of abbreviated heading whose initials need not be given full stops: those whose initials can be, and usually are, pronounced as if they formed a single word, like UNESCO. These are frequently used as the main entry headings, so that the omission of the stops allows no confusion with other main headings in small capitals.

The second justifiable use of full stops in indexes is in cross-references. Like all parts of the index, cross-references should be punctuated as lightly as possible. With the simplest of simple cross-references there should be no punctuation at all. Until recently most indexes adopted one or other of the following forms

Animals. *See* Livestock.

Animals, *see* Livestock.

Animals. *See* Livestock

Animals, *see* Livestock

the last two being compromises resulting from the fairly recent discontinuance of the ending of all entries with full stops. But the only logical stopping place is the completely unpunctuated form

Animals see Livestock

which is adequate and unambiguous and has fewer characters to check. It is the cross-reference 'see also' which is sometimes preceded by a full stop. This is when it runs on from numerical references on the same line, as explained in the chapter on Cross-references (IX d) and illustrated in the following example

Chichester, bishops of, 3, 152, 617. See
also Arundel, John; Peacock,
Reginald; Story, Edward

The full stop after the final numerical reference is appropriate because it is firmer than the preceding commas and also than the subsequent semi-colons. But when 'see also' begins a new line, usually at the end of the entry, there should never be a full stop at the end of the preceding subentry. Finally, the abbreviated cross-references 'cf.' and 'q.v.' always have full stops as shown here.

(c) *Colons*

Colons should be used only after main headings, and even then they are essential only in two special circumstances when there are two or more modifications. First, the main heading should be separated by a colon from the first modification in paragraphed entries when there are no numerical references following the unmodified heading. In the following example

Debts: acknowledged by sealed bonds,
161; distraint for, 22, 192; liberties
of Hanse merchants concerning,
555-8; pleas of, 53, 161, 374; settled,
134; statutes merchant executed for
non-payment of, 3

the colon makes it quite clear that all the modifications relate to 'Debts', whereas if a comma is used instead some users might assume that the second and subsequent modifications refer to 'Debts, acknowledged by sealed bonds'. In fact, if that were the case no comma would be necessary after 'Debts', although in other cases there can be genuine ambiguity. Secondly, inverted subject headings should be followed by a colon when the first modification continues on the same line, even though subsequent modifications begin with new lines. Thus

Seals, episcopal: applied to charters, 67
forged, 59, 72
matrices of, 153

is far clearer than the use of commas throughout could conceivably make it under the indentation system which is recommended later (XI b-e). But place names which are inverted require no colon because the inversion creates no ambiguity if the rules set out in the chapter on Places (III b, n) are followed. Indeed, in

Norton, Chipping, Oxon, 532

a colon between 'Chipping' and 'Oxon' would be absurd. If anywhere, it should be placed after 'Oxon', since the county (and in other cases a parish, supplied or not) is an integral part of the main heading, to the whole of which all subsequent modifications relate.

This suggests the question: if colons are recommended for certain headings, why should they not be used after every one—subject headings, full place names and surnames—whether they have one modification, more than one or none at all? There are indexes in which they are, and these certainly have the merit of consistency. But the colon is a very heavy mark of punctuation to appear after every heading, especially when numerical references immediately follow it, as the following short example cannot adequately show

> suicide: 30, 92, 543
> Sutton Vautort (Sutton, Sutton Viu-
> tort, Vautard) [in Plymouth],
> Devon: 75, 150
> Sutton: John, 181
> John de, 233

Possibly because of this some authorities recommend that no punctuation be used before the first reference of an entry or subentry, but that it should be separated from the preceding word by an extra space thus

> suicide   30, 92, 543
> Sutton Vautort (Sutton, Sutton Viu-
> tort, Vautard) [in Plymouth],
> Devon   75, 150

But that is to go too far to the other extreme, and it also increases the difficulty of checking the proofs. The ideal punctuation after headings is a comma, except in the two situations described above in which colons are to be preferred. The slight inconsistency is unimportant, particularly as headings end at widely different points across the column, as our last examples show, and so do not create either a vertical column or any pattern.

It follows that there is one type of index in which colons need never be used, although they sometimes are. It is that whose headings, and sometimes some subheadings also, stand on a line of their own. Even more unnecessary is a colon followed by a dash, which is occasionally found after such headings and sub-headings as the following

> Ships:-
> (*here follow modifications*)
> types of:-
> (*here follow types of ships*)

When neither references nor a modification run on from a heading or sub-heading, there is no justification for adding any punctuation at all, since normal indentation adequately indicates that the modifications relate to the whole of the heading or subheading from which they are indented.

(d) *Semi-colons*

Semi-colons are recommended for three situations only. One is to separate subentries in entries arranged in paragraph form, as is shown in the 'Debts' example in the last section and in others below (XI d). In such entries commas are used in the normal way (see next section), which makes necessary a heavier kind of punctuation at those points at which a new line would have been started in any other arrangement. Semi-colons have exactly the right weight. We will see (XI d) that it is occasionally desirable for long entries to be divided into two or more paragraphs. All such paragraphs except the last should end with a semi-colon to show that there is more following which relates to the same main heading. This is useful because although, as will be shown, second and subsequent paragraphs are always indented, a searcher in a hurry may assume that the end of the first paragraph is the end of the entry. The semi-colon should alert him to the fact that it is not. There should be no punctuation at the end of last paragraphs or of entries, the vast majority, which consist of only one.

The second use of the semi-colon is to separate two or more persons, places or subjects cross-referred to by the words 'see', 'see also' and 'cf.' In our earlier example

> Chichester, bishops of, 3, 152, 617. *See*
> *also* Arundel, John; Peacock,
> Reginald; Story, Edward

the superiority of the semi-colon over the comma, which is the only other possible type of punctuation in this situation, is obvious. Not only are commas needed to separate surnames from forenames, just as they are similarly needed to separate the two elements of inverted place names or inverted subject headings, but semi-colons more firmly indicate that the separated items are or contain main headings to be sought individually. The one exception to this use of the semi-colon is when there are multiple cross-references from modifications in entries arranged as paragraphs. A lighter punctuation is essential in such lists because semi-colons are used to separate the modifications (see X c, d; XI d). The items cross-referred to can therefore only be separated by commas; and, indeed, if 'see also' is used it must be preceded by a comma instead of the usual full stop. But cross-references should not be included in the middle of paragraphed entries unless there is no alternative. Fortunately they can usually be avoided, as explained elsewhere (XI d).

When alphabetically adjacent entries, usually obsolete or variant forms of a place or surname, are jointly cross-referred from, as discussed above (III c; IX b), they are separated by commas, as in

> Berwyck, Berwycke, Berwyk *see* Ber-
> wick

whereas when two different modern names share one obsolete form the corresponding composite cross-reference uses semi-colons, for example

> Haghton *see* Haughton; Hawton

This may appear inconsistent, but in fact it is not. Only alphabetically adjacent forms are jointly cross-referred from, so that even if the first name is inverted (subsequent ones need and should not be) there is no ambiguity resulting from the use of commas throughout. Moreover, we have earlier recommended that such cross-references be normally to and from just the words of substance (III c). By contrast, the names jointly cross-referred to are hardly ever alphabetically adjacent. Often they are far apart, and the semi-colon emphasises their separateness and difference: that they are distinct entries to be looked up individually. It may be thought that the semi-colon introduces too strong an element of separation: that the second name, Hawton, in our last example appears not to depend on 'see', and that there should therefore be lighter, not heavier, punctuation between Haughton and Hawton than after Haghton. But such composite cross-references are rarely numerous. They certainly never occur so frequently as to warrant the invariable use of a full stop before 'see'. The fact that 'see' is in italics is probably sufficiently arresting to make a full stop unnecessary, while a comma before 'see' would be of no advantage because it is weaker than the semi-colon. The other alternative—replacing the semi-colon with a comma—would be suitable if all such cross-references were to single words. But commas are required to separate the two parts of inverted names, which necessitates heavier punctuation between the different names themselves. It is rarely necessary to give full cross-references to composite place names. Usually a cross-reference to the words of substance, as in

Hoton *see* Howton; Hutton

is adequate, although occasionally it may be thought desirable to give the names in full, for example

Hoton *see* Howton; Hutton, Sand

and then the merits of the semi-colon stand out. Moreover, if a comma is used to separate two subjects which are being cross-referred to and which would naturally relate to similar matters, the second could easily be interpreted as a subentry of the first, as it genuinely is in cases such as

Borough customs *see* Law and Customs, borough

The slight demerits of the semi-colon, which are not such as to mislead or even delay the intelligent searcher, are therefore outweighed by its advantages, which include the merit of consistency with cross-references to persons, as illustrated in the Chichester example above, in which semi-colons are essential.

Thirdly, semi-colons are recommended for separating the references to the different volumes in indexes which cover more than one, as in the following

Barnard, Clement, II 188, 216; III 54;
IV 22, 334; VI 176

More about such entries will be found above (VIII b; X b).

(e) *Commas*

In every index there are many more commas than there are full stops, colons and semi-colons put together. They will be found in almost every example in this work, and many of their uses have already been mentioned in this chapter. In short, whenever some punctuation is required and a full stop, colon or semi-colon would be inappropriate for reasons suggested above, a comma is almost certainly the answer. Commas precede the first reference of any entry or sub-entry and separate any subsequent references; they come both before and after the inverted sections of headings, subheadings and modifications; and in the type of modification which refers back specifically to the word or words of the heading, subheading or previous modification, a comma must always be inserted at the point at which the heading would be repeated, as in the following example

Castles, 6, 9, 20, 78
    bridges of, destroyed, 67
    exchequers of, records in, 17

The commas here are important both to indicate the order of the words and also in case any further modifications of 'bridges' and 'exchequers' were required. In that case a further indentation would relate only to the words in the previous line up to the first comma, for example

Castles, 6, 9, 20, 78
    bridges of, destroyed, 67
        rebuilt, 199

Here the bridges which were rebuilt had not been destroyed, or at least this fact is not given in the index entry. It is because of this use of the comma—to separate that part of a subheading or modification which is repeated by subsequent indentation from that which is not—that it is advisable not to omit commas before or after brackets if they would be inserted in the absence of brackets.

In persons and places entries commas should be used in accordance with the above rules, with normal grammatical conventions and with common sense. Thus

Cooden (Coding) in Bexhill, [Sussex],
29

is correct. There are commas each side of the county, despite the fact that it is in square brackets (see X g), because it is not preceded by a preposition. Likewise there is no comma after the second round bracket because Cooden is linked to Bexhill by the word 'in'. Some indexers always use a comma between the lesser place and the parish, presumably to show that the second name is the parish in which the first place lies and that they do not form a single place name like Weston in Gordano or Sutton in Ashfield. There are several reasons why this possibility of confusion need not be taken seriously and accordingly why the comma is superfluous. First, the great majority of parishes are supplied by the indexer and are therefore in square brackets. Secondly, for most centuries there will be obsolete forms of nearly all places, and these always precede the parish but in the case of composite place names follow the whole name: for example Weston in Gordano (Westone). Finally and most important, searchers turning to a particular place in the index may be assumed to know its form sufficiently well not to be misled.

Persons entries can be more difficult.

Pedley, John of Nottingham, 66
Pilling, Henry and Mary his wife, 98

are both wrong. There should be commas after 'John' and 'Henry' since their names, like all personal names in indexes except for those indexed under forenames and those, such as Mary in the last example, who are described in terms of others, are basically inversions and whatever follows them is by way of definition or additional information.

Popinjay, Henry, Mary, wife of, 133

has one comma too many, after 'Mary', although it is often erroneously inserted, as is a comma after 'Mary' in the previous example. Both are excessive, and 'Mary, wife of' is disruptive of immediate understanding, since one of the main purposes of a comma in an index is to relate the word or words preceding it to an earlier word or words—something which should be done for the whole phrase 'Mary wife of'.

It is not possible to mention here every use, and misuse, of the comma. The numerous examples in the chapters on Places, Persons and Subjects cover most of them. But as cross-references have already been discussed in connection with semi-colons (X d), it must be noticed here that 'q.v.' cross-references to lists of persons and places use only commas throughout, as in

Plymouth, Devon, 78, 194
Sutton Pool, Sutton Prior and Sutton
Vautort in, q.v.
Bentley, Hooper and Spicer of, q.v.

and when lists of fields and other minor place names are followed by direct references they also are separated by commas. This is all considered in detail, with examples of other usages which are not recommended, earlier in this work (III e, i, j; IX e).

(f) *Inverted commas*
Inverted commas should be used as sparingly as possible, and double inverted commas never. Single ones can conveniently be placed around field and other minor place names which are unidentified or have not survived in a modern form, to distinguish them from those given in modern forms. (For examples see III i.) Similarly, larger places which are completely unidentified or for which possible identifications are only tentatively suggested in square brackets after the obsolete forms, have to be indexed under the obsolete forms, and it is better that they should be in inverted commas than in italics which are sometimes used because

'Powfold' (unidentified), 27

although it may at first sight appear to be slightly indented (see the fifth example in X g), forms a more satisfactory typographical contrast than

Powfold (unidentified), 27

More about this usage, with examples, will be found elsewhere (III g; XI i). For similar reasons, although titles of books and journals, and names of ships and inns are best printed in italics, as explained in the next chapter (XI i), books especially can occasionally be printed in romans in single inverted commas if the typographical context makes it desirable.

(g) *Brackets*
Square brackets are reserved for the enclosure of matter which is not in the text, but has been supplied from other sources by the editor. It is generally matter which would have been incorporated in the index in the same place, but without the brackets, if it had been in the text. Parishes and counties are most frequently printed in square brackets, as is fully described and illustrated in an earlier section (III f). As is there stated, square brackets should never surround the first word or words of an entry. Thus the supplied family names of peers and bishops (see IV m) should not be in brackets. Again, they should not be used if there is just a single reference in which all the information is provided in the text, although some of it is missing in all the others. Any opportunity for dropping the brackets must be grasped. (For more on this see III f.)

A slightly different use of square brackets is shown in

'Hoton' [?Houghton], Yorks, 152

where they embrace a possible identification of a Yorkshire place about which there is a large measure of doubt (see III g). Similarly, whereas

Page, [George], 27

means that the forename has been omitted from or is illegible in the manuscript but that there is no doubt what it should be,

Page, [?George], 27

means that in a similar case it is almost certain that it is George but with the slight possibility that it could be someone else. When there is considerable doubt or no clue at all, the index entry must, of course, read

Page, ..., 27

Other uses of square brackets, including the enclosing of dates for peers with identical names (see IV m) and places and counties in which other identically named persons were active (IV n), will be found in earlier chapters.

Round brackets have several uses in indexes to record publications, the most commonly occurring being the enclosure of the obsolete forms of places and the variant forms of surnames immediately after the modern or chosen spelling in the main entry heading (see III c, d; IV b). They are similarly used for obsolete or variant forms of street, field and other minor place names in subentries (III i). Other uses are exemplified in the chapter on References: they surround page numbers or numbers of subentries in references to entries which run on for several pages of the text, so that the entry number alone is insufficiently specific, and also numbered footnotes; and they enclose such explanatory words as *'bis'* when there are two, or more, casual mentions of the same person, place or subject on the same page (VIII a, c, e). Indeed, apart from their use for obsolete and variant forms, round brackets are mostly employed to enclose explanatory matter. Many explanations resolve possible confusion; others point out difficulties that remain. But they rarely incorporate firm information derived from sources other than the text for which square brackets are normally reserved. The following are typical examples, and others will be found at relevant points throughout the book.

> Smith, John, of Derby, 76
> John, of Derby, (*another*), 227
> 'Aston' (*unidentified*), 69
> Brewer, James (*once called* John), 17,
> 22, 99-103
> Baxter, William, and Jane (Marsh) his
> wife, 152

Marsh in the last entry being Jane's maiden name (see IV l).

Finally, as already mentioned incidentally (X e) and also illustrated in this and other sections, punctuation (it is usually a comma) should not be omitted when it is immediately followed or preceded by a bracket. It is true that in the entry

> Cooden (Coding) in Bexhill, [Sussex],
> 29

the commas next to the square brackets, and especially the first one, are not absolutely essential, although their inclusion, if inconsistent with our rule that punctuation should be kept to a minimum, is consistent with another—that punctuation should be used consistently. In other cases, however, the comma helps in the easy comprehension of the significance of subsequent indentation. For example, in the entry beginning

> Walker, [Alan], Joan wife of, 17
> Lawrence brother of, 6
> Benjamin, 22

Lawrence is clearly Alan's brother, but if the commas were omitted he might at a quick glance appear to be Joan's.

CHAPTER XI
TYPOGRAPHY AND LAY OUT

(a) *Repetition by Typographical Symbols*

There are several methods of presenting complex index entries. One is to use some typographical symbol to represent repetition of the main heading and, when necessary, of a subheading and/or modification also. One such symbol is a single comma, used as follows

Martin, Elizabeth wife of William, 322,
714
, John, 588, 561
, Roger, 337
, , bailiff of Northampton, 32,
834
, , , deputy of, 572
, William, 322
, , wife of *see* Elizabeth

More frequently double commas, ditto marks, are used, while, until very recently, the Pipe Roll Society used double commas separated by single ones, so that it would have printed the above entry in this way

Martin, Elizabeth wife of William,
322, 714
,, , John, 558, 561
,, , Roger, 337
,, , ,, , bailiff of Northampton, 32,
834
,, , ,, , ,, , deputy of, 572
,, , William, 322
,, , ,, , wife of *see* Elizabeth

None of these usages is recommended, mainly because they all lack clarity. The use of rules, or dashes, is clearer:

Martin, Elizabeth wife of William, 322,
714
– , John, 588, 561
– , Roger, 337
– , – , bailiff of Northampton, 32,
834
– , – , – , deputy of, 572
– , William, 322
– , – , wife of *see* Elizabeth

Some indexers use rules without commas, which is slightly less clear, others use a double rule (two dashes) for each repetition, which is of no greater assistance, while a few adopt the indefensible practice of printing as many rules for each repetition as there are words in the heading, subheading or modification repeated. By this last practice the middle of our example would run

– , Roger, 337
– , – , bailiff of Northampton, 32,
834
– , – , – – – , deputy of, 572

But if one is going to employ a typographical symbol to indicate repetition, the most satisfactory is a row of dots. It is normal to use six for repetition of the main heading and four for each subheading or modification, as follows

> Martin, Elizabeth wife of William, 322,
>> 714
> . . . . . . , John, 558, 561
> . . . . . . , Roger, 337
> . . . . . . , ... , bailiff of Northampton,
>> 32, 834
> . . . . . . , ... , ... , deputy of, 572
> . . . . . . , William, 322
> . . . . . . , ... , wife of *see* Elizabeth

(b) *Repetition by Indentation*

The second main method of presenting such entries is to use indentation instead of typographical symbols, each repetition being indicated by an indentation to the right. The indentation should be uniform, and it is suggested that each should be of either two or three spaces, but that run-on lines of main headings or of first modifications which themselves run straight on from headings should be indented four or six spaces, while all other run-on lines should be indented two or three spaces to the right of the first line from which they run on.[1] By this system our example would be printed thus

> Martin, Elizabeth wife of William, 322,
>> 714
>> John, 558, 561
>> Roger, 337
>>> bailiff of Northampton, 32, 834
>>> deputy of, 572
>> William, 322
>> wife of *see* Elizabeth

Some variations of this type of lay out are sometimes encountered. One is for the main heading to stand on a line of its own, either printed normally or in small capitals, and this will be considered later (XI f). Another is for each subheading or modification to be so arranged that it begins immediately to the right of its heading, as follows

> Brown, John, 17
>> William, 223
> Brownlow, Anthony, 542
>> Clement, 312
>> William, and Anne his wife,
>>> 16
> Bryant, Alice, 27
>> Matthew, 716
> Butterworth, John and Robert, 319
>> Stanley, 76

This has the advantage of making the heading stand out particularly clearly and of showing immediately to exactly which word or words the subentries relate.

---

[1] The spacing mentioned here and elsewhere in this chapter is for the guidance of the indexer as typist, although, as the examples given throughout this work show, the relative degrees of indentation apply to indexes in print.

But it has two great disadvantages. The lay out of the index as a whole is rendered completely irregular, each entry forming its own vertical column of subheadings and modifications at a different point across the column according to the length of the main heading or its key word. Equally important, much space is wasted, particularly with entries with long headings or key words, when the subheadings and modifications can begin very far to the right, as happens with places such as

Kingston Bagpuize (Kingstone Bagpuss),

Berks, 156

manor, 223

bailiff of, 167

For both reasons this lay out is not recommended.

(c) *Symbols and Indentation*

When one compares the indentation system at its best with the best of the usages employing typographical symbols—that with dots—each is found to have its advantages. The latter is sometimes clearer. Modifications which continue into a second or even a third line (although three lines should rarely be necessary) can all begin at a fixed point along those lines, normally indented four or six spaces, without any possibility of confusion with the subsequent modifications or subheadings which are all introduced by dots. By contrast, if the first line runs on in the indentation method, it is indented four or six spaces, which obviates any confusion with the first subentry; but lack of width in index columns means that a subentry which runs on must often start its second line only two or three spaces beyond its own indentation, so that any modifications which may follow stand out less clearly, and sub-subentries present even greater problems. Indeed, the indentation method is less flexible, because the number of possible indentations is smaller than the maximum possible number of series of dots. This is because each indentation limits the width of the run-on lines, whereas run-on lines are unaffected by the number of sets of dots in the other method.

A second situation in which the use of dots is clearer is illustrated by the following example

Winchelsea, Sussex, manor, 838

. . . . . . , ... , reeve of, 632

The second set of dots immediately shows that the reeve is the reeve of the manor of Winchelsea. In the other usage this could be indicated by a double indentation thus

Winchelsea, Sussex, manor, 838

reeve of, 632

town walls of, 18

but only when, as here, it is followed by a singly indented subentry. If there were no further subentry the double indentation would not be readily apparent, and the normal practice in such circumstances is to indent only singly thus

Winchelsea, Sussex, manor, 838

reeve of, 632

In the same way

Holland, George, 67

John son of, 263

Richard, 32

is correct, with John doubly indented, but if there were no other Hollands following, he would be singly indented thus

Holland, George, 67

John son of, 263

This is perfectly clear and satisfactory, but the last Winchelsea example is ambiguous. The reeve could be either reeve of the manor or reeve of the town, whereas in the two preceding examples he is manifestly reeve of the manor. It may be argued that such confusion is comparatively rare and hardly ever of the first importance: that very few people will be interested in the reeve of the manor and not in the reeve of the town, or *vice versa*. But from this standpoint it could be maintained that the exact form of many an index entry is not vitally important taken by itself, and yet the value of an index as a whole depends upon the complete reliability and intelligibility of all the separate entries.

There are considerations, however, which have resulted in the almost universal replacement of the use of typographical symbols by the indentation system. It is more aesthetically pleasing, it is more economical of space and, most important, it is easier to set up in type. It should always be possible to eliminate ambiguity by rewording. Thus our Winchelsea entry could be recast to read

Winchelsea, Sussex, manor, 838

reeve of the manor, 632

It should also be possible to rearrange complex entries to enable them to fit into the indentation system. If it is not, there is almost certainly something fundamentally wrong with the entries. Subdivisions of sub-subentries are to be avoided. They confuse more than they assist, and they are a sure sign that the entry is too complex and should be broken up into its main elements.

In order to save excessive indentation some indexers repeat the main heading for each of its major subdivisions. This has the grave disadvantage that many searchers, on reaching a repeated heading, will not look closely but will merely assume that an entirely new entry will follow, thereby possibly missing many valuable references. Others number the subheadings of very long entries. This certainly facilitates cross-reference to them, but does not solve the difficulties of lay out. Indeed, when entries are long but not abnormally complex, a long series of subentries can be mistaken for a column of main entries. In such cases there is no objection to combining the best of the two systems, showing that the main subheadings are only subheadings by preceding them with a row of dots, but indenting their modifications. Rigid consistency must always give way to clarity.

(d) *Paragraphed Entries*

There is a third method of setting out index entries. Where space is particularly short, all entries can be printed in paragraph form. Most space is, of course, saved in volumes devoted to records in which a few important persons and places constantly recur, or in volumes of local records in which the county town and other places come up in many contexts and a large number of people share relatively few surnames. The most simple type of paragraphed entry might begin

Smith: Adam, 22; Alan, 634; Bertram,

34, 75; Colin, 615; David, 522-30;

Denis, 64; Edmund, 502; Edward,

63, 66, 207; Francis, 78; George, 23,

78; Gregory, 95; John, 32, 66, 78,

It is sufficient, and saves much space, to indent the run-on lines only two or

three spaces. Modifications should be separated from each other within subentries by commas, not semi-colons, thus

> Smith: Adam, 22; Alan, 634, wife of
>   *see* Constance; Bertram, 34, 75;
>   Colin, 615, bailiff of Sutton, 22;
>   Constance wife of Alan, 634, 700;
>   David, 522-30; Denis, 64; Edmund,

Some individuals come up in so many different offices, or otherwise qualified,
that they warrant their own paragraphs, like Edward Smith in the following
example, in which to save yet more space common forenames are abbreviated in
the manner recommended in the chapter on Persons (IV k). It is, of course, in
indexes set out in paragraph form that such abbreviations are most frequently
encountered. Incidentally, in entries consisting of more than one paragraph all
run-on lines should be indented four or six spaces and the first word of the
second and subsequent paragraphs two or three spaces.

> Smith: Adam, 22; Alan, 634, wife of
>   *see* Constance; Alex, 65; Bart, 6;
>   Bertram, 34, 75; Colin, 615, bailiff
>   of Sutton, 22; Constance wife of
>   Alan, 634, 700; David, 522-30;
>   Denis, 64; Edm, 502;
>   Edw, 63, 66, 207; bailiff of Easton,
>   303; escheator in Nottingham-
>   shire, 55, 87; steward of the abbot
>   of Westminster, 422; under-sher-
>   iff of Nottinghamshire, 11;
>   Francis, 78; Geo, 23, 78; Greg, 95;
>   Jn, 32, 66, 78, 123, 324, 418, 500;

There is one slight disadvantage in this lay out, in that it appears at first sight as
if the subentries in the paragraph beginning with Francis should all be modifications of Francis in the same way as the preceding paragraph relates entirely to
Edward. But if the paragraph method is used throughout the index the user
should not be misled for more than a moment. The alternatives have graver
disadvantages. To include Edward in the middle of one long paragraph, with his
various offices separated by commas, would allow much more confusion: it
would be easy for a user to go back to Edmund, for example, rather than Edward
in his desperation at trying to ascertain who held these various offices, especially
with the forenames abbreviated. The other alternative is not to indent the lines
below Francis. It is true that the name Francis would then stand out less than
Edward, but the resulting block of entries is aesthetically displeasing. Moreover,
any subsequent Smith paragraph, for example for a William Smith, would also
not stand out as much as Edward's paragraph, even with its run-on lines indented;
and as such a paragraph would relate to a single complex person similar to
Edward this lack of clarity and lack of uniformity would be quite serious. This
is our last example so arranged and extended

> Smith: Adam, 22; Alan, 634, wife of
>   *see* Constance; Alex, 65; Bart, 6;
>   Bertram, 34, 75; Colin, 615, bailiff
>   of Sutton, 22; Constance wife of

Smith (*contd*)
>   Alan, 634, 700; David, 522-30;
>   Denis, 64; Edm, 502;
>   Edw, 63, 66, 207; bailiff of Easton,
>   303; escheator in Nottingham-
>   shire, 55, 87; steward of the abbot
>   of Westminster, 422; under-sher-
>   iff of Nottinghamshire, 11;
>   Francis, 78; Geo, 23, 78; Greg, 95; Jn,
>   32, 66, 78, 123, 324, 418, 500; Mat,
>   59; Mic, 39, 44; Nat, 119; Nic, 2;
>   Phil, 112; Ric, vicar of Newton,
>   339; Rob, of Norton, 29; Rob, of
>   Sutton, 6;
>   Wm, 33, 126, 515; alderman of Not-
>   tingham, 42, 67; mayor of Not-
>   tingham, 444; sheriff of Notting-
>   ham, 159-61

A minor variation of this lay out is to indent the whole of the paragraph following a 'block', so that the last seven lines would appear as follows

>   Phil, 112; Ric, vicar of Newton,
>   339; Rob, of Norton, 29; Rob, of
>   Sutton, 6;
>   Wm, 33, 126, 515; alderman of
>   Nottingham, 42, 67; mayor of
>   Nottingham, 444; sheriff of Not-
>   tingham, 159-61

but this makes little difference to the clarity of the entry as a whole. On balance, therefore, the lay out of the first multi-paragraph example is to be preferred to any possible alternatives, one of which involves repetition of the main heading which was considered and dismissed in connection with other types of entry (XI c). Some might like Alan and Colin to have small paragraphs of their own, but that hardly seems necessary. Exactly what length of subentry makes a separate paragraph desirable is a matter for each indexer's discretion.

A few points concerning paragraphed entries may be usefully brought together here, although most are considered at greater length in other chapters. First, in our example the main heading is followed by a colon, and this must be done whenever the heading is not followed immediately by a reference, in order to make it clear to what word or words subheadings and modifications refer. (For further examples see X c.) Secondly, subentries are separated by semi-colons, which are also used at the end of all paragraphs but the last in those complex entries which consist of more than one paragraph, in order to alert the user to the fact that the next paragraph does not begin a new, and irrelevant, entry. Thirdly, modifications of subentries should be used as sparingly as possible and, unless the subentry has its own paragraph, should be separated from the subheading and from each other only by commas. Because of this it is advisable that subject entries should be simpler than is necessary in other types of index, and that as many modifications as possible should refer to the main heading. All such modifications should form a single paragraph and should be followed by any subheadings, each beginning a new and indented paragraph containing its own modifications. It is recommended as a general rule (V g) that, whatever the lay out, modifications of subject headings should precede subheadings rather than that they should all be merged in a single alphabetical sequence, but this is particularly desirable in paragraphed entries. Fifthly, the wording of all paragraphed entries should be simpler than in those whose modifications are arranged line by line, and inversions should be avoided (V f). Finally, cross-references from subentries should be kept to a minimum and everything should be done to avoid multiple cross-references, since the various headings referred to cannot be separated by semi-colons which are reserved for the different context and weightier emphasis described above; but to separate them by commas, the only alternative, has disadvantages already detailed (X d). If it is absolutely essential to have cross-references in the middle of a paragraph, they can only be separated from the subentry from which they refer by a comma and can only have commas within them. But every effort must be made so to organize cross-references that they all come at the end of the entries, if necessary in a separate paragraph of their own.

Just as the other two methods of lay out of index entries—by the use of typographical symbols and indentation—can be combined, so paragraphing can be used in conjunction with either of them. Dots can usefully be introduced into a paragraphed index at the beginning of second and subsequent paragraphs of the same entry, and could have been so used in our Smith example. This is the equivalent of their occasional use in very long entries in an indented index (see XI c). Equally, paragraphs can usefully be employed in what are basically line-by-line indexes, whether dots or indentation are used. The most usual way of doing this is to begin all subheadings and single modifications of main headings on new lines, but to run on all modifications of subheadings and all second modifications, thereby forming paragraphs, although often very small ones, as in the following example

> Law courts, extortion practised in, 179
>   held in castles, 66, 391
>   records produced as evidence in,
>   314, 442
>   types of
>   borough, 16, 39, 156, 412; held in
>   Guildhall, 315; views of frank-
>   pledge held in, 51
>   Common Pleas (Bench), 398, 526;
>   fines levied in, 62, 199, 333
>   county, 15, 98, 423; outlawries in,
>   q.v.

Similarly in our Smith example every individual would begin a new line, all but the first being indented two or three spaces, while all modifications of particular men would run on to form paragraphs. In the last version Alan and Colin, as well as Edward and William, would have paragraphs of their own rather than have their modifications further indented as in the full indentation lay out, and all the other individuals would begin a new line. Semi-colons are not needed at the end of any paragraphs since the basic arrangement is not by paragraphs.

Occasionally one encounters paragraphed indexes wherein each paragraph block is situated immediately to the right of the main heading or its key word, however long or short it may be. This sort of lay out has already been deprecated when applied within the indentation system (XI b). It is even less appropriate with paragraphing because, aside from its irregular appearance, it is extremely wasteful of space which it is the sole merit of paragraphing to save.

(e) *Symbols, Indentation and Paragraphing: a Summary*

The various methods of lay out discussed above may be summarised as follows. The use of dots, the best of the typographical symbols, is slightly the clearest, but often uses most space and is the most costly, for which reasons it has largely fallen into disuse. Indentation has the most pleasing appearance. Paragraphed indexes are the most difficult to use, both because they lack clarity compared with those set out line by line and also because their subheadings, modifications and cross-references are greatly restricted by the format so that they are frequently less pointed and specific than one would wish. Nevertheless paragraphing saves space and it is therefore quite often the only lay out possible if a comprehensive index is to be printed. Finally, the compromise of combining the paragraph system with one of the other two can be a happy one, especially when only sub-subentries are run on. Such a combination gives some saving of space without sacrificing the clarity of the line-by-line arrangement.

For the greatest possible clarity, all examples in the other chapters of this work are set out with every subheading, sub-subheading and modification on a line of its own, except, of course, in those cases where a heading, subheading, sub-subheading or modification is followed by no numerical references and the first (or second) modification runs straight on. The indentation system is also used throughout because it has almost completely replaced the other line-by-line systems.

(f) *Small Capitals*

In most indexes the successive indentation of subentries and sub-subentries adequately shows their hierarchical position, and no typographical differentiation of headings and subheadings is needed. Indeed, if every heading is printed in either small capitals or bold type, as is sometimes done, the effectiveness of the emphasis is destroyed by too frequent use, and the searcher has to make an almost conscious adjustment when reading from one type face to another. Similarly, the recommendation, to be found in some works on indexing, that large capitals, small capitals, bold type and italics be used in that descending order of emphasis to distinguish respectively headings, subheadings, sub-subheadings and subdivisions of the last is strongly opposed here. If there are also modifications indented from each category of heading, the entry is too large and complex and should be split up (see V b; VI a). Only main headings should ever need typographical emphasis, and very few even of them.

In some indexes there will be a few entries which are longer, more complex and more important than the rest, and they can be justifiably emphasised typographically. The most pleasing way of doing this is to print the heading in small capitals, but this should only be done when the heading stands on a line by itself, as is the invariable practice throughout some indexes and as is the practice for many of the subject entries in others. Indeed, the longer and more complex entries are more likely to be subjects than persons or places, and the longer and more complex they are the more likely it is that their headings occupy a separate line anyway. We have already seen (V f) that it is unimportant that a few subject headings, usually those of grouped or general subjects, are on a separate line while the rest are followed immediately by references or modifications. The further slight inconsistency that the first group of headings, or some of them, are in small capitals is equally unimportant. A separate line and small capitals are also useful, often more so, for the headings of the few outstandingly important persons and places in General Indexes which attract numerous subject modifications (see VI a). But the practice, sometimes encountered, of using a different typographical device for each different kind of entry in a General Index—small capitals for places, bold type for persons, and so on—is quite unnecessary, and, indeed, is confusing rather than helpful.

(g) *Bold Type*

There are some occasions when it is desirable to emphasise a heading which is followed on the same line by references or a modification. In such cases bold type, with only the first letter a capital, looks better than small capitals throughout. Italics have many other uses (see XI i), and so they should never be used to emphasise headings. Bold type is often used for persons who have a special significance, for example those who are the subjects of inquisitions *post mortem* or coroners' inquests in volumes devoted to such records. A typical entry might read

Beauchamp, Henry, 77, 94
John, 12, 54, **94**
Richard, 122

the reference to the inquisition on John Beauchamp and John's forename also being distinguished by bold type. This method of emphasis is superior to all alternatives, such as changing the alphabetical and numerical orders to

Beauchamp, John, 94, 12, 54
Henry, 77, 94
Richard, 122

for reasons already given (VIII d). There will rarely be circumstances in which other selected headings or references need special typographical emphasis: an appropriately worded modification is usually the best way of drawing attention to them. In some indexes covering more than one volume the volume numbers are printed in bold arabics, but it has been shown above (VIII b) that large roman numerals are preferable and that bold type is unnecessary.

(h) *Initial Letters*

All headings of persons and places entries must, of course, begin with capital letters. Also in a Subject Index it looks more natural for each key word to begin with a capital. There would be no point in beginning every one in the lower case. But in order to differentiate them from persons and places and to make them stand out, it is advised that subject entries in General Indexes be printed entirely in the lower case, with the exception of the few which are given small capitals and any beginning with or consisting of words which are invariably begun with capitals (see VI a).

The subheadings and modifications of every kind of entry in every type of index should begin with small letters, except for those beginning with or con-

sisting of proper nouns or words which always require capitals and for subheadings of some entries whose main headings are in small capitals. One occasionally
finds indexes in which subheadings and modifications are arranged alphabetically
by the first significant word without any inversion, prepositions and other
unimportant words being ignored, and in which attention is attracted to the
significant words by giving capitals to their first letters. That system of alphabetising is not recommended (see VII b), and this use of capitals which some of
its practitioners find necessary is a further argument against it. One also encounters indexes in which, when main headings are inverted to bring the most
significant word to the beginning, the first word of the natural order is given an
initial capital; and the same is even occasionally done with inverted modifications. But simple inversions should not need to be so marked, and if more
complex ones do they are too complex and should be simplified.

(i) *Italics*

Italics serve many purposes. They should normally be used for the titles of all
published works; for the names of ships and inns; and for foreign words and
phrases, which in indexes to record publications are most frequently the Latin
names of writs and of personal and place names. They are also used for the
words of direction in all cross-references, as is fully illustrated in the sections
devoted to that subject (IX b-f). Similarly, words of explanation such as normally appear in round brackets are often italicised: words such as '*now in*' or
'*formerly in*', '*unidentified*', '*once called*', '*two men*', '*another*', '*bis*', and so on.
Examples will be found in most of the foregoing chapters, but notably in III g,
IV n, VIII e and X g.

But the effect of italics is considerably impaired by excessive use. It is therefore
advisable to avoid long runs of entries or subentries in italics. If, for example,
under the subject heading 'Writs' there is a long list of subentries each consisting
of the Latin name of a particular writ, there is a strong case for printing them in
roman rather than in the usual italic type. Similarly, a long list of printed books
would probably be better in roman type, with each title within single inverted
commas—a practice which some indexers adopt for printed works anyway.
Again, italics should not be used for different purposes for adjacent words or
phrases. Thus in the long entry headed 'Ships' used earlier in this book (V g)
there occurs the line

Trinite, la, (two ships), 276, 594

The contrast between the italic and roman type is far more effective than if
italics are used throughout thus

Trinite, la, (two ships), 276, 594

Here the point of the italics is lost, although both uses of them are individually
correct. For the same reason it is recommended (III g) that completely unidentified place names be indexed under their manuscript forms in single inverted
commas,

'Powfold' *(unidentified)*, 27

being typographically clearer than the uncontrasted

Powfold (unidentified), 27

and being more satisfactory than

Powfold (unidentified), 27

because the last is inconsistent with the treatment of unidentified field and other minor place names, all of which are normally printed in single inverted commas because their numbers would otherwise render many indexes over-italicised (see III i). But

Certiorari see under Writs

may sometimes be the best usage.

Certiorari see under Writs

is no improvement, and

Certiorari see under Writs

although much the clearest, could be slightly misleading as it would encourage the user to expect to find the subheading '*certiorari*' under 'Writs' in roman type. If, indeed, it is, because it is one of a long list of writs, there is no problem and the last cross-reference would naturally be used.

Some authorities advocate the use of italics for dates, but there is no justification for this as a general rule. In such an entry as

Jacobite Rebellion of 1745, 399

they are a slight help in contrasting the date with the reference, although italic and non-italic arabic figures are fairly similar so that

Jacobite Rebellion (1745), 399

is much clearer. There is no case for italicising dates when they are added in square brackets merely to distinguish persons of the same name (see IV m) or to make more explicit the chronological arrangement of an entry (VI a). Even less justifiable is the printing of dates in bold type, as is sometimes advised and done. Such explanatory aids should be less, not more, prominent than the rest of the entry.

Some record societies have recently experimented by publishing volumes reproduced by offset-litho from typescript, which is cheaper than conventional letter-press printing. The typewriter used should always have italics. Under-lining is too heavy and clumsy in appearance to be an adequate substitute, particularly in the index, and the omission of both italics and underlining limits the range of typographical emphasis at the editor's disposal. Record publications should be meant to last for all time, and there are therefore limits beyond which economy measures should not be pressed.

(j) *Space between Letters*

When an index is set up in print it is helpful to have a small space, the equivalent of four or five lines, between the last entry of one letter and the first of the next. A greater amount of space is merely wasteful, and no useful purpose is served by printing the new letter in the middle of the column in the space or by having a larger than usual initial letter for the key word of the first entry of the new letter.

(k) *Run-on Entries*

At the page-proof stage it is necessary to ensure that the headings, and any relevant subheadings, of entries which run on from one column of index to another are repeated at the top of the second column. They must never be merely represented by dots or rules, or, even more meaningless, by indentation, which will only be recognised as such when the next entry or subentry begins. In some very long entries that may not be until the third column is reached, so that the subentries in the second column will appear to be main headings. A simple example of what is required must suffice. Let us assume that in the entry beginning

> London, 3, 51, 58, 158, 237
>> churches in
>>> All Hallows, Gracechurch Street,
>>> 3
>>> St Antholin, 51
>>> St Christopher le Stocks, 145
>>> St Clement, Candlewick Street,
>>> 125

the last-named church had to begin a new column. That column would have to begin with the main heading and subheading repeated, as follows

> London (*contd*)
>> churches in (*contd*)
>>> St Clement, Candlewick Street,
>>> 125

and this whatever the position of the column and not just if it is the first column of a left-hand page. The first two lines are often printed

> London — *contd*
>> churches in — *contd*

but we have already seen (X g) that explanatory words are normally enclosed in round brackets and there is no reason to depart from the practice in this case. To save a line the first two lines can be combined in some such way as this

> London, churches in (*contd*)

which is adequate, although slightly less clear and rendering it possible that the subsequent churches may be indented to an incorrect extent.

It is essential to ensure that a main heading, subheading or modification does not straddle two columns. Thus if in our example the last line had started a new column, one of two things must be done: either a line must be saved in the first column by rearrangement of the type, so that the last line can be made the last line of the column, an extra line being made in the second column; or both the St Clement lines must go to the top of the second column, one line being saved somewhere there and another being made for compensation in the first column. With paragraphed entries it is inevitable that in some cases there will be a run on from the foot of one column to the top of the next. This is yet another disadvantage of that system, and all that can be done is to repeat the main heading at the top of the second column on a line of its own, as it might be

> Smith (*contd*)

CHAPTER XII

THE INDEXER AND HIS TECHNIQUE

(a) *The Indexer*

One theme which has underlain the greater part of the preceding chapters is that the editing of records for publication and the indexing of the resulting volume are not completely separate activities but must proceed hand in hand. From his first thoughts about the form of the volume to the completion of the text the editor must keep the index in mind. As has been seen (VIII a), the editor must try to arrange his text into entries of a length suitable for index references. In short, there is an overwhelming case for the editor and the indexer being one and the same person.

The indexing of persons and places, especially places, is much more efficiently done by the editor than by another person. We have already recommended that, irrespective of indexing considerations, every place should be identified by the editor in the case of calendars and descriptive lists and printed in its modern form in the text (III d); and for transcripts he has frequently to identify places, and often persons also, in order to confirm the forms in which they occur in his manuscripts: to be certain of readings where the manuscript is faded or decayed, and to decide how a number of consecutive minims should be split up into letters or even whether two minims should be rendered as 'n', 'u' or 'v' or 'ii'. Having identified his places and persons for the establishment of his text, the editor will save time in the long term by indexing them on cards straight away. Not only that, but for many editor-indexers there are psychological advantages in indexing the persons and places either entry by entry or in small groups of entries as the text is prepared. There are then a number of fully edited and largely indexed entries to show for each day's work, only the Subject Index and the inevitable editing of the Index of Persons and Places being left to the end. In this way the more interesting and the more tedious parts of the editor-indexer's work rapidly rotate, and he is kept more alert by the diversification of activity. Alertness, awareness and perception of associations are essential qualities for an editor and an indexer, but they can be rapidly blunted and his work can become routine, mechanical and pedestrian through over-lengthy concentration on one aspect of it.

Another argument for indexing the persons and places of each entry immediately or shortly after it is prepared is that the references are then much more likely to be written down accurately, whereas when one indexes a long series of entries one after the other it is very easy to continue to write the number of the previous entry after one has moved on to the next. Finally, indexing always brings to light some errors in the text, and the sooner they are discovered and corrected the better.

The indexing of persons and places, although never easy, is nevertheless basically a matter of applying a number of firm rules, but the compilation of Subject Indexes, or the subject element of General Indexes, requires different qualities and skills and a far wider range of knowledge and experience, particularly in order to recognize conceptual subjects or subjects which appear under unusual words or are only obliquely indicated in the text. This is one of the reasons why it is often suggested, notably by professional indexers, that indexes should not be compiled by the authors or editors of the books. Another argument is that some other person is much more capable of making the objective analysis of the text which is essential for a balanced index. But these arguments hardly apply to record publications, even to their Subject Indexes. Carried to their logical conclusion, they would disqualify the editor from writing an Introduction to his volume, and we have already seen (V a) that the Introduction and the Subject Index should be dovetailed as complementary sections of the publication. No mere indexer can ever acquire the same intimate knowledge of the records as the editor who has transcribed or calendared them; and in the case of a calendar or a descriptive list only the editor will know the exact relationship between the original manuscript and his text. He is therefore best qualified to index the subjects as well as the persons and places. Moreover, being a record scholar or archivist, he will normally be at least as well acquainted with indexing techniques as any professional indexer.

(b) *Preparation of Indexes: Order of Work*

The different requirements of indexing persons and places on the one hand and subjects on the other determine the order in which the work is done. We have already seen that the indexing of persons and places is comparatively straight-forward: they have all to be included, their occurrences in the text are always obvious and there are firm rules for their treatment, so that they can be indexed either entry by entry as the text is prepared or at least so frequently that no text is left unindexed at the end of a day's work. By contrast, subjects are less obvious and their treatment inevitably varies from volume to volume, so that a knowledge of much of the text is often essential before the pattern and nature of the Subject Index can be gauged. Hence subjects do not lend themselves to the same early treatment. Not only that, but the Subject Index gains considerably if it is prepared in a single uninterrupted operation after the text has been completed. It thereby attains a greater consistency than it would otherwise have. The order in which the various parts of a record publication should be prepared is therefore: first, the text and the Index of Persons and Places concurrently, the latter being edited at any convenient later stage; second, the Introduction; and third, the Subject Index.

(c) *Preparation of Indexes: Writing, Sorting and Editing Cards*

This is a large topic, but fortunately it has been exhaustively treated in most of the works on indexing listed in the Bibliography and so it can be dealt with fairly summarily here. Because all indexes to record publications are large, the use of cards is essential. The word 'card' is used in this section to cover good quality paper cut to card size, which is usually much cheaper. A convenient size has always been five inches by three, and of the newly introduced metric sizes the most useful will probably be A7 (74 by 105 mm.). It is also helpful to have a filing cabinet, or at least some drawers, in which to keep them, and some guide cards, preferably of a different colour, with tabs standing above the level of the index cards, to flag the main divisions of the index. There should be guide cards at the beginning of every letter at least, and in larger indexes the longer letters such as 'B', 'H', 'M', 'S' and 'W' will need to be subdivided. In many indexes it is also useful to have guide cards to mark the beginning of important entries, such as 'London', the leading persons or the main subjects.

Every person and place should be clearly ticked, struck through or in some other way marked on the manuscript or a carbon copy of the typescript of the text as it is written on a card. So should every specifically mentioned subject, although some of the less concrete subjects do not allow of this treatment. By thus marking his text the indexer can later verify that no person, place or specified subject has been omitted from the index. Each person, place and subject should be written on a separate card, as should the various modifications of the same heading. This saves a great deal of rewriting at the editing stage, since one can never be sure how many modifications an entry may ultimately have, and there will often prove to be insufficient room for all of them in any space left on a single card or the spaces will be in the wrong positions alphabetically.

Every person and place mentioned in the text must be indexed, and most of their subheadings and modifications will be obvious at the card-writing stage. Subjects are more difficult because they vary in importance, and therefore often in their hierarchical position in the index, from volume to volume. It is consequently important not to impose a preconceived or arbitrary pattern upon the Subject Index from the outset. Each specific subject should be individually indexed in the first place, with any necessary modifications, until eventually the main groupings are suggested by the specific entries themselves. In a series of volumes it should be possible, as well as desirable, to adopt the classification of the first volume for subsequent ones, and with certain types of records some of the subject groupings become obvious at a very early stage. But otherwise it is preferable to classify the entries at the end, when all the cards have been written. The best thing initially is to write a card for every conceivable subject and modification. Some subject cards will inevitably prove unnecessary later, but it is far easier to remove them than, realising too late that certain subjects have been omitted, to be forced to go through the text again. Similarly some modifications will prove to be excessive or too general, but once again it is simple to strike them out, merely adding the reference number to the unqualified heading. It is tedious and time consuming to have to look up big entries again in order to break them down into manageable sections. It may also be mentioned here that whenever, in writing subject cards, a synonym comes to mind, a card should be written cross-referring from the synonym to the heading with the references. In this way reasonable cross-references are less likely to be omitted and subjects are less likely to be split up under different headings.

After the indexing of each entry the indexer should glance quickly through the resulting cards to ensure that all have been given a reference and that it is the correct one. No indexing errors are easier to commit and harder to rectify, or in the case of the first even to recognize, at a later stage than the writing of wrong references (most frequently that of the preceding entry) or the omission of them altogether.

The decision as to how often to sort the cards into the main index in their correct alphabetical positions is a very personal one. There are two extremes. Some indexers do no sorting at all until the last entry has been indexed, preferring to concentrate for an unbroken period on each activity in turn. The drawback to this is that the task of sorting is thereby greatly augmented because there are separate cards for every occurrence of every person, place and subject, except for those few which every indexer keeps by his side to add to, knowing that they figure constantly in the text. There will even be a large number of repeated cross-references, unless all cross-referring is left to the final editing. The other extreme is to sort the cards into the index entry by entry immediately after they are written. The advantage of this is that new cards need never be written if one knows that a particular heading, or heading and modification, has occurred before. One merely turns to its alphabetical position, aided by the guide cards, and adds the new reference, and sometimes a new obsolete or variant form; and, of course, one can still keep the very popular cards at one's elbow. In this way the size of the index during its compilation can be kept within bounds. Nothing is more daunting than to be faced with drawer after drawer of ever expanding cards. But if the entries in the text are short, as they should be, to sort the cards into the main index after each one is indexed involves too frequent changes of occupation. The best thing is almost certainly to sort all the new cards in at the end of each session of indexing, or at least at the end of each day. Thereby any inefficiency resulting from too frequent switches is obviated. One can transcribe, or calendar, and index for long spells and then, when one is getting tired and liable to error or inexactness, turn to the less demanding task of sorting and, of course, of transferring the references from any duplicated entries onto the earlier cards. Then, when one returns to the job refreshed the next day, all the existing cards will be in alphabetical order.

It may be necessary to have a slightly different system for the Subject Index from that used for persons and places. Subjects are usually fewer in number, but many will occur in the text much more frequently than most persons and places. It is therefore helpful to sort the subject cards into the main alphabetical sequence at shorter intervals, so that they may be added to during indexing, than those recommended above which are appropriate for persons and places. Such frequent sorting is also an aid to consistency, which it is much more difficult to achieve for subjects.

In those rare cases when it is impossible for the text to be arranged by entries and the index references therefore have to be to pages, the cards should still be written before the text is printed, and preserved in the text order so that the references can be added at the page-proof stage. This is a check that everything is indexed, although it produces a very large number of cards for the final sorting.

When every card has been written and is in its appropriate alphabetical position, the work of editing can begin. Almost certainly the most obvious result of this is that the index will visibly shrink. Many cross-reference cards can be removed because they lie adjacent to the entries to which they refer; and others can be conflated because they are alphabetically adjacent forms of the same name or place for which one cross-reference will therefore serve (see IX b). Many modifications will prove unnecessary and can be deleted, the references being added to the main headings or appropriate subheadings. Others will prove too elaborate and will have to be simplified. Complex subject entries may have to be recast, or sometimes split up, which in its turn will necessitate further cross-references. This stage may also disclose a few errors of transcription. It may be realised, for example, that John Bacon must be a misreading of John Baron. If it proves to be so, the text can be corrected accordingly. Not every eventuality encountered in editing an index can be mentioned here. But, in general, the editing stage should ensure a uniformity of treatment and a consistency of tone. It is the time at which to make all entries as simple as possible, while ensuring that no aspect of importance is omitted. Another essential part of editing is to verify that there are no loose ends, and especially that all the cross-references direct the user to an entry which has specific references. All this involves much rewriting and some resorting. It is therefore very easy for single cards, or even whole runs, to escape from strict alphabetical order, and this in turn can on occasions result in a duplicate series of entries: as serious an indexing crime as dispersing references to an identical subject under synonymous headings about which a warning is given earlier (V c). This, then, is the point at which to check that all the cards are still in strict alphabetical order.

The remaining task is to mark the cards in such a way that the lay out desired is clear to the printer or, more usual these days, to the typist; and it is safer not to neglect it even if the indexer knows that he will shortly become the typist himself. He must see first that the heading is clearly set out on the first card of each entry, and secondly that it is boldly struck through on all subsequent cards: a single diagonal stroke in pencil is the most effective. Similarly, when sub-headings are repeated they are struck through in the same way. Thus one diagonal stroke indicates that the remaining words on the card are to be indented beyond the heading, two strokes indicate double indentation, and so on. Last of all, the cards should be numbered on the back with an automatic numbering machine. It is a tedious job, but it ensures that a typist who drops a bundle can rearrange them without necessarily understanding the principles on which indexes are compiled. The cards should be retained after they are typed and the galley proofs checked against them rather than against the typescript, so that any errors in the typescript which escape notice are not perpetuated. Finally, at the page-proof stage there is the need, already described and illustrated (XI k), to ensure that the top of every column of index which begins with part of an entry running on from the previous column is adequately headed.

SELECT BIBLIOGRAPHY

Bancroft, R., 'Some Requirements of Good Indexes', *Library Association Record*, vol. LXV (1963)

British Records Association, *Notes for the Guidance of Editors of Record Publications* (1946)

British Standards Institution, *Alphabetical Arrangement* (B.S. 1749: 1968)

British Standards Institution, *Recommendations for the Preparation of Indexes for Books, Periodicals and Other Publications* (B.S. 3700: 1964)

Brown, G. E., *Indexing: A Handbook of Instruction* (1921)

Carey, G. V., *Making an Index* (Cambridge Authors' and Printers' Guides, no. III, 3rd edn, 1963)

Clarke, A. L., *Manual of Practical Indexing*, 2nd edn (1933)

Collison, R. L., *Indexes and Indexing*, 3rd edn (1969)

Johnson, C., *The Mechanical Processes of the Historian* (S.P.C.K. Helps for Students of History, no. 50, 1922)

Knight, G. Norman (ed.), *Training in Indexing* (Cambridge, Mass., 1969)

Petherbridge, Mary, *The Technique of Indexing* (1904)

Quinn, J. H. and H. W. Acomb, *A Manual of Cataloguing and Indexing*, 2nd edn (1937)

'Report on Editing Historical Documents', *Bulletin of the Institute of Historical Research*, vol. I (1923-4)

'Report on Editing Modern Historical Documents', *ibid.*, vol. III (1925-6)

Walsh, J. W. T., *The Indexing of Books and Periodicals* (1930)

Wheatley, H. B., *How to Make an Index* (1902)

Wheeler, M. T., *Indexing: Principles, Rules and Examples*, 5th edn (New York, 1957)

Golden valley - trees. Steep roofs & stone & slate
Chapels. White woodwork. Big houses on hill
top. Jumble of jaderaised cottages at Chalford
Old mills + modern factories. Weeds + waste
Elsen floor. Multi storeyed mills, decaying + lopsid
Rush filled canal bed. crossed by bridges
Remains of Halts. Clear towpath + river
water. Houses by the towpath. meadows.

Stroud rising in brick + Welsh slate
Elder: hawthorn + willows.

Stroud Rly proclaiming proudly on the deserted
goods shed ' GWR STROUD STATION ----

Paneurym station with fresh paint

.

From Hampfield - trees catching green Cotswolds
in late sun, each crowned with gold quarry sal ?
  Past Haresconibe + ⊞ of Pinkward
Pinkward